Relish
my Life in the Kitchen

by Lucy Knisley

:01
First Second
New York

How do you remember things? What are your clearest memories?

I like to think that I have a good memory, especially for stories. I enjoy *telling* them and remembering how things unfolded.

My most vivid memories consistently jog my brain with the recollection of how things *tasted*.

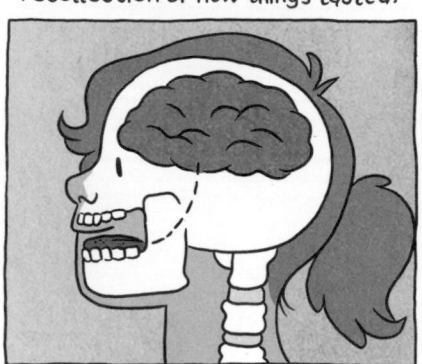

I'm lucky to have grown up with cooks and bakers, eaters and critics, and meals to remember. My memories were formed in conjunction with my palate, collected along with photographs of shared meals from my childhood.

IN

How can I remember my first crush, without recalling the taste of the licorice rope we slung between our mouths, the marshmallow waiting in the middle for the winner?

How could I ever remember my childhood best friend, without bringing to mind the sour taste of buttermilk, simultaneously gulped without the benefit of being able to understand the packaging?

Taking my vitamins in the morning reminds me of the sweet, chalky taste of the jar of Flintstones I snuck, in an act of delicious medicinal rebellion, eaten like candy, inches from the television screen.

PLEH!

Walking down the street of my neighborhood in Chicago, I pick up the smells of fresh tortillas, slow-cooking bratwurst, basil growing in a nearby window box; each stimulates the taste recollection of a time, a trip, or a person.

Sometimes it's frustrating, this selective memory. I can remember exactly the look and taste of a precious honey stick, balanced between my berry-stained fingers, but my times tables are long gone, forgotten, in favor of better, tastier memories.

The book you're reading contains a collection of my favorite stories, crammed with the taste-memories that draw them up through my mind from years ago.

I hope that you find your own appetite piqued, and you remember a time you tasted something that would shape you for years to come.

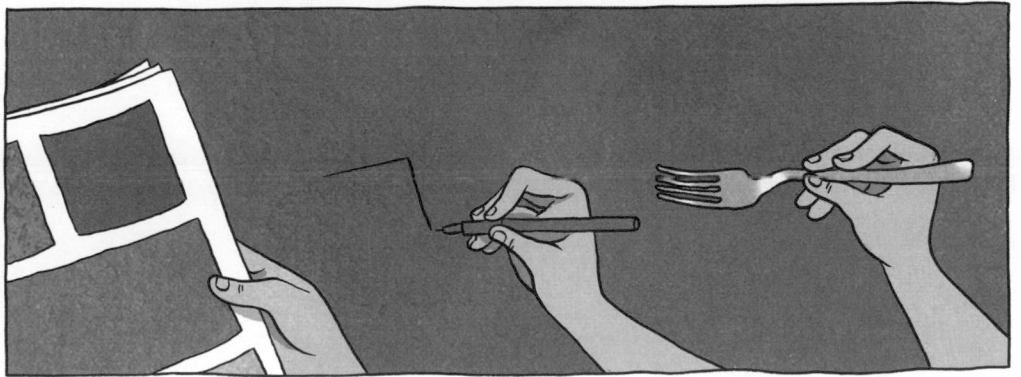

SPICE TEA

🍂 SOMETIMES KNOWN AS CHAI! 🍂
THIS IS DELICIOUS STUFF — CAFFEINATED AND WARM (OR ICED!)

YOU'LL NEED:

THESE SPICES ARE GREAT, BUT THIS WILL WORK EVEN IF YOU DON'T HAVE ALL OF THEM.

VANILLA EXTRACT

MAPLE SYRUP

CINNAMON

ANISE STARS

CARDAMOM PODS

CLOVES

BLACK TEA

IN A DIFFUSER

OR

BAGGED

MILK OR SOY OR OAT OR ALMOND MILK

A STRAINER

→ OR A VANILLA BEAN

GINGER (FRESH OR DRIED)

PUT 2-3 CUPS WATER IN A SMALL POT ON THE STOVE ON HIGH.

ADD 2 BAGS OR A DIFFUSER OF BLACK TEA AND LET IT HEAT UP.

BURBLE!

BREW!

MEANWHILE, CRUSH 3 CARDAMOM PODS WITH THE SIDE OF A KNIFE.

GRATE OR CHOP ABOUT ½ TEASPOON OF GINGER.

BLADE AWAY FROM PALM

SQUISH!

BE CAREFUL!

← FINGERS UP

OR MORE, DEPENDING

ON YOUR TASTE.

TOSS IN:

1 ANISE STAR

1 VANILLA BEAN (OR CAP OF EXTRACT)

THE GRATED GINGER

1 CINNAMON STICK

6-8 CLOVES

THE CRUSHED CARDAMOM

AND STIR!

STIR WHILE IT SIMMERS, UNTIL IT HAS A SOUPY CONSISTENCY (USUALLY 5-10 MINUTES).

GET READY FOR YOUR HOUSE TO SMELL LIKE CHRISTMAS.

LET COOL FOR A BIT, THEN STRAIN IT INTO A LIDDED GLASS CONTAINER.

(YOU CAN REUSE THE CINNAMON STICK AND VANILLA BEAN, BUT CHUCK THE REST OF THE STRAINED-OUT STUFF.)

MAPLE SYRUP

ADD MAPLE SYRUP TO TASTE...

AKA, LOTS

POUR OVER MILK (OR MILK SUBSTITUTE), ABOUT ½ MILK, ½ TEA MIXTURE.

← MILK

IF THE MIX IS STILL HOT, IT'LL WARM THE MILK—IF NOT, NUKE IT!

CAP AND REFRIGERATE TEA MIXTURE FOR LATER USE (LASTS ABOUT A WEEK). (YOU CAN ALSO FREEZE IT FOR LONGER.)

& ENJOY YOUR TEA

COOKIE WARMED BY TEA STEAM

CHAPTER 1

THE *Kid* IN THE *Kitchen*

I was a child raised by foodies.

My parents probably don't recall how old I was at my baptism, but they remember what I ate that day.

Poached salmon in cream

Poofy baptism dress

I couldn't have asked for a better godfather than a renowned restaurant critic.

After all, my family worships nothing so much as we do food, and the trinity of cooking, dining out, and eating.

When I was seven, school birthdays always meant cupcakes, but *my* mom brought a <u>blowtorch</u>!

There, on the dinosaur table, while my classmates watched in awe, she caramelized sugar on an enormous crème brûlée.

For a time, Mom worked at the restaurant of David Bouley, doing flower arrangements and helping in the kitchen for events.

From my spot on the floor, I could charm the waitstaff and sous chefs.

Back then, she could bring me, so I'd spread out my coloring books and sit while she cut lilies or prepped sauces.

Want a profiterole, kiddo?

My favorites were the truffle mice! (These are still made in NYC by Larry Burdick.)

We lived in a strange, old converted factory in downtown Manhattan.

The former residents had split in a nasty divorce, prompting the furious wife to use olive oil to write "Fred Stell is a drug addict and drag queen" in enormous letters on the brick of the kitchen wall.

Every night, my dad and I would make the salad dressing for dinner. He would stand at the worn butcher block in the kitchen, and boost me up on a chair.

There, I had an excellent view of my mother's mysterious spice rack.

what do these strange powders do!?

Dad would pour out a capful of Kressi vinegar and hand it to me, careful not to spill.

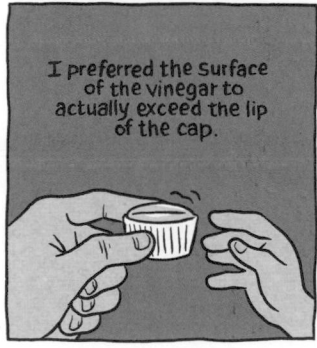

I preferred the surface of the vinegar to actually exceed the lip of the cap.

I would toss back my shot of vinegar like a hardened pro, and Dad, grimacing, would do the same.

We mixed the vinegar with Dijon, salt, olive oil, and a clove of garlic that Dad would crush with the heel of his palm against the butcher block.

crunch

9

Around the corner from our apartment was my uncle Peter's shop. The Peter Dent Store was a little food shop on N. Moore and Hudson. He sold an assortment of gourmet comestibles and homemade food.

Pete's store was a beautiful little place: pressed-tin ceilings, columns, and enormous barrels of olives and cornichons, too high to reach on my own.

Pete employed a raggedy team of talented artists and rockers to chef the kitchen.

Quite a few of them were in late-80s punk rock bands, and often their art took priority over the running of the store.

Sorry, Pete. We got a gig...

Pete's then-girlfriend did the flower arrangements for many of the nice restaurants in New York. I remember watching her in the alley behind Pete's kitchen while she coated a selection of leaves with shining gold spray paint while singing along to Patti Smith on the kitchen's radio.

My uncle Peter was the one to first teach me about oysters. I love the way eating oysters is like consuming cold liquid metal, the way I imagine the TI-83 robot from the Terminator would have tasted, but saltier.

Peter took a netted bag of lumpy brown rocks, and showed me how to perform the alchemy to unlock their secrets.

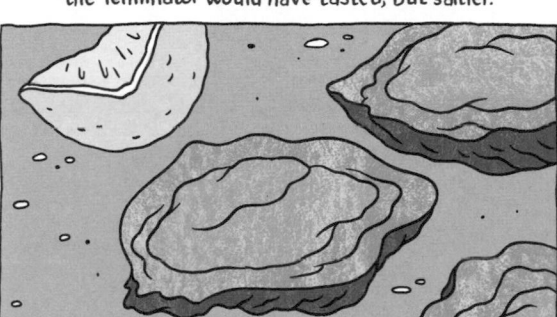

Patiently, he showed me how to hold my oyster in a nest of dish towel, and pry the butt of the oyster with the tip of my knife. When it reluctantly opens, your triumph is carefully tempered by the effort not to spill the precious oyster brine.

It takes too much muscle for me to have been much good at it when I was younger. But now I can almost match Peter in his speed and precision.

This is tested at nearly every family gathering, when Peter and I shuck oysters until our hands are numb and our clothes smell like the ocean.

(And I've got the scars to prove my years of practice.)

I think we have enough oysters...

My mother's friends, artists and chefs, would get together regularly to throw dinner parties where they'd try their hands at cooking something new.

Shelley Boris, a painter and chef, who went on to head the kitchens at The Garrison

Ray Bradley, a farmer and former chef who helped form the New York farm-to-table scene, and whose dinners at his beautiful upstate farm are legendary.

Maureen Higgens, amazing baker.

Terry Jampol, who moved to Costa Rica and opened a great bed and breakfast.

The other kids and I would run through the kitchen, usually in some state of undress, while our parents and their friends laid the table with amazing things.

This tradition led to an annual Easter party. Every year at her house in Rhinebeck, NY, my mother hosts this event, to which she invites her friends and colleagues, filling the house and yard with chefs, bakers, restauranteurs, and caterers.

The resulting meal is so enormous and delicious that the party has occurred annually for over twenty years now.

Early on, before the Easter party got too big for the house and expanded to the yard, we used to have a sit-down dinner. I remember one particular Easter, during which my mother focused her theme on French cuisine.

Does that mean we can make chocolate mousse?

can we?

please?

The culinary guests brought enormous soufflés, duck confit, and traditional French bread baked that morning. But the crowning dish of the meal was my mother's appetizer of braised foie gras on a bed of home-grown arugula.

It was my first exposure to the fattened goose liver (not that I knew what it was), and having eaten all of my own, I set out to make the rounds of the table. At each chair, I begged the remainder of each guest's serving, with a pleading, gap-toothed smile.

But I didn't usually spend my childhood cracking my spoon against a Wednesday crème brûlée...

...More often, I was serving it.

I readily admit that I may have been terribly spoiled when it comes to food, but it comes from being "the help."

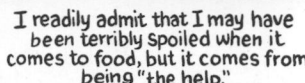

Great job tonight, kids.

Looks like there's plenty of cake left over for us!

I feel incredibly lucky that the work my family has done has given me so many good things to eat and cook and experience.

An array of delicious memories that have stayed with me, flavoring my childhood.

CRACK

THE DENT · FAMILY · PATENTED MARINATED · LAMB

MY MOM'S FAMILY HAS MADE THIS LAMB AT SPECIAL EVENTS SINCE MY GRANDMOTHER USED TO PREP IT, AND MY GRANDFATHER WOULD GRILL IT AFTER WORK IN THE SIXTIES.

Aunt Heidi

Uncle Harry

Uncle Peter

SNAP

← Mom

A BUSINESSMAN AND THE SON OF AN INVENTOR, MY GRANDFATHER DIED SHORTLY AFTER I WAS BORN.

WHEN MY FAMILY COOKS TOGETHER— ESPECIALLY THIS DISH— MY MOTHER AND HER SIBLINGS CAN REMEMBER HIM CLEAREST; JOKING WHILE HE CARVED THE LAMB, COOKED JUST RIGHT.

YOU'LL NEED

A BUTTERFLIED LEG OF LAMB
(YOU CAN ASK FOR THIS CUT
FROM YOUR BUTCHER. THEY
DE-BONE THE LEG AND OPEN
IT UP. IT'S USUALLY ABOUT 5 LBS)

(Don't let
actual
butterflies
get near it.)

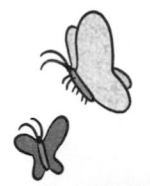

SOY
SAUCE

GARLIC

FRESH
MINT

ROSEMARY

WHITE
WINE

KIKKOM
SOY

OLIV
OIL

HONEY

OPTIONAL SIDES

COUS·COUS   GREEN BEANS

1. PEEL & CRUSH "MANY" (8-10) CLOVES OF GARLIC, AND RUB THEM ON LAMB. THEN STREW THEM OVER THE LAMB AND PAN.

SQUISH

2. SMEAR ALL OVER WITH OLIVE OIL, THEN RUB MINT AND ROSEMARY OVER LAMB, AND PLACE UNDERNEATH.

RUB RUB

3. POUR 1 CUP OF SOY SAUCE AND 1 CUP OF WHITE WINE OVER THE LAMB.

GLUG GLUG

4. DRIZZLE A THIN LAYER OF HONEY OVER THE WHOLE SHEBANG.

WHEE!

5. LET THIS MARINATE FOR SEVERAL HOURS, TURNING OCCASIONALLY

FLIP!

SPLOOSH

Either

GRILL OVER HOT COALS

OR

ROAST IN A HOT OVEN (450°)

'Till RARE!

THIS RECIPE ISN'T FOR PEEPS WHO LIKE WELL-DONE LAMB — SORRY!

AFTER 30 MIN, TURN OVEN TO 375°

THIS TAKES ABOUT 30-40 MINUTES, DEPENDING ON MEAT/METHOD.

CAREFUL! THE HONEY & FAT CAN MAKE THE COALS FLARE UP.

FOOM!

EeK!

SOME CHARRING IS GOOD, BUT YOU DON'T WANT IT TOTALLY BURNED.

WHEN DONE, MEAT THERMOMETER SHOULD READ 130°-135°

BE SURE TO LET IT *REPOSE* AFTER REMOVING IT FROM HEAT (AT LEAST 20 MINUTES)

IT WILL COME UP TO 135°-140°

Tic Tic

RESIST THE URGE TO CUT BITS OFF! YOU'LL LET OUT THE JUICES!

SIGH. PATIENCE.

SLICE & SERVE!

YAY!

CHAPTER 2

COUNTRY HOUSE · CITY MOUSE

When my mother took me, at seven years old, to live in the beautiful countryside of upstate New York, I was unamused.

Manhattan child as I was, I could not imagine a world that wasn't divided into blocks and boroughs.

My mother took it upon herself to acclimate, while I sulkily mourned my former proximity to FAO Schwarz.

We'd moved to the country when my parents divorced, so my mom, determined to forge a life of independence and nature, dragged me along on her little-house-on-the-prairie fantasy.

She planned a magnificent vegetable garden, and we trooped all over the Hudson Valley to countless seed and plant stores.

I can't imagine a more incredibly boring place for a kid than those garden stores; reeking of fertilizer and potting soil and never without a scowling, child-hating clerk.

During one of these yawn-inducing outings, my mother was taking a particularly long time over garden gloves, when I reached my limit.

Furious, I stormed out of the store, crossed the parking lot to the dirt road, and with great force and determination, flung my hand into the air, screaming:

If there had, in fact, been a taxi passing by on that wooded dirt road, I could have returned safely to New York. That would've shown her!

My mother's vegetable garden flourished, yielding wonderful things:

Asparagus, basil (for fresh pesto), cherry tomatoes, zucchini in staggering numbers, baby lettuce, tomatillos (which I'd peel and eat hot from the vine, crunchy and delicious, after unwrapping them like pieces of hard candy).

My section of the garden (tended almost entirely by my mother) was full of nasturtiums.

The flowers are bright fire colors, and edible! They turned salads into spicy, colorful, delicious flower gardens!

THERE'S A SLUG ON THIS ONE!

Well, get rid of it!

For the things she couldn't grow, my mother turned to Greig Farm.

A small family farm nearby.

I liked the farm store, where I could buy a handful of honey sticks (closed straws filled with honey) for a dollar, and eat them while I (unhygienically) petted the dairy goats that were penned nearby.

Maybe the country isn't so bad...

After practicing on a rubber glove with pinholes in the fingertips, I was allowed to milk the goats and pour the cream into jam jars, which I shook until sweet, soft butter formed.

In Greig's strawberry season, we'd pick berries in the fields for market.

And Mom made jam until the whole house smelled so good that I floated around in a near-drunken stupor.

The cooking berries would simmer in enormous pots on the stove, volcanic and fragrant, scenting the house with the damp, warm sweet/sour smell that settled like a blanket over everything.

I'd find creative uses for the leftover berries that we didn't sell or jam.

Mom →

placed very carefully on the table

There was a small pond near the berry-picking fields, where I slowly learned to skip rocks and catch frogs.

A flock of enormous white geese prowled the edges of the water, their vicious serrated beaks parched for my blood.

When I wandered too close to their nests one day, they began to rear their heads with malicious hissing. I backed away, but by then it was too late!

The country is home to many creatures that can harm an unwary city kid; coyotes, bobcats, rabid raccoons... But nothing has ever sprung upon me with the violent intent of those geese.

Honking and hissing, they chased me up a tree right into a hornet's nest.

Stung on the eyelid, I flailed off of my branch, and into some fragrant farm mud...

THUD

... where I was easy prey for the geese, and they had at me with hissing, honking delight.

I eventually broke free and survived to tell the tale, but spent the rest of the day with a halved onion on my eye, to draw out the hornet stinger.

*$#/ing country!

I have since eaten foie gras with great enjoyment and very little guilt.

Soon after we settled into the country life, Mom began to work at a farmers market, selling for Greig Farm and some local dairies.

Her market partner was a man named Kip, who introduced us to Osage oranges.

(Also known as horse-apples, bois d'arc or bodark)

Osage trees grow all over the Hudson Valley. They have incredibly odd, bright green, brain-like fruits the size of grapefruits.

They're mostly ignored by the tree owners, except when they have to mow their lawns.

Augh!

They're inedible, but have a sweet citrusy scent and make wonderful (and fragrant) decorations.

Kip carves beautiful wooden bowls from the Osage tree's wood.

Kip seemed to know every spot in the Hudson Valley where one could obtain a free harvest. The Osage oranges we sold at market were often plucked from the lawns of Kip's unsuspecting neighbors.

Getaway truck

This was also how we obtained goldenrod, pussy willow, and a fruit that Kip called "goldenberries" for market.

Otherwise known as Physalis, or "the lost fruit of the Incas," they're raspberry-sized semi-sweet objects that grow encased in lantern-like husks.

On goldenberry-harvesting excursions, we'd pluck them from bushes on the side of the road, or from the backyard of a local resident who hadn't the sense to appreciate them in time.

Like sweet, yellow cherry tomatoes!

Once in a while, the lawn owner wasn't too pleased with our scavenging, and a few times we had to get out of there quickly.

Don't drop the berries!

SORRY! SORRY! SORRY!

But Kip would creep back as soon as their cars pulled out, escaping with buckets of the little yellow fruits in their papery jackets.

DANGER berries!

I got better, bending my city-kid self to the country, but never quite reached that status of the true farm kid, where animal mortality is accepted as a part of life.

The chickens raised from peeping handfuls to vicious pecking monsters would get eaten by raccoons, and I'd be traumatized.

The neighbor kid

The dog would drag home a leg of a deer that he found on some roadkill monstrosity...

...And I'd look at him differently from then on.

And I'd have nightmares for a week after wandering into my mother's catering refrigerator, only to find that our neighbor was using it to store the results of his latest hunt.

AUGH

Yum!

But I think it changed my relationship to the world, to my body and food, to see that what I ate didn't originate on the shelves of a store.

After all, the city might have exquisite food, but I'm certain that no restaurant in Manhattan can match my mother's pesto, still warm from the sun on the basil leaves.

I'll never forget learning that you can eat corn right off the stalk!

why do we even bother cooking this!?

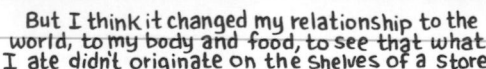

MOM'S PESTO

≈ GET TOGETHER ≈

A FOOD PROCESSOR...

ROMANO & PARMESAN

OLIVE OIL

PINE NUTS

GARLIC

SALT

...STUFFED WITH FRESH BASIL LEAVES

COMBINE

GARLIC CLOVES

2 HANDFULS PINE NUTS

BIG HANDFUL CHEESES

"A BIT" OF OLIVE OIL

"LOTS" OF SALT

ADD MORE OIL AS THE PROCESSOR PROCESSES

UNTIL IT BECOMES A THICK PASTE.

WRRRRR

ENJOY ON TOAST, VEGGIES, OR...

...PASTA!

PESTO TIPS & IDEAS

DANG, IT'S GOOD ON EVERYTHING!

BE SURE TO USE GOOD, CHUNKY SALT!

ADD CHERRY TOMATOES TO PESTO PASTA!

A BIT OF LEMON ADDED TO PESTO KEEPS IT BRIGHT GREEN LONGER!

TOAST
SALT
TOMATO
PESTO
GOAT CHEESE

♥ SNACK! ♥

♥ IN SALAD DRESSING! ♥

1 PART DIJON
1 PART BALSAMIC
1 PART OLIVE OIL
1 PART PESTO
A PINCH OF SALT
A SQUIRT OF LEMON

♥ ON MOZZARELLA, TOMATO & BALSAMIC ♥

ON AVOCADO!

ON CUCUMBER!

BASICALLY IT MAKES ANYTHING DELICIOUS!

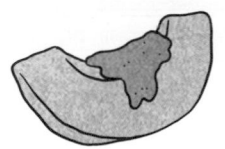

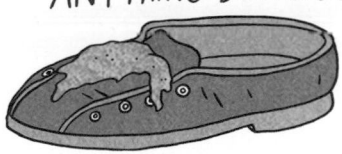

CHAPTER 3

TOUGH COOKIE

For a period of time, my mother and I kept chickens in our backyard.

The coop

They were mostly Rhode Island Reds; particularly vicious red-brown birds that laid small, beautiful coffee-ice-cream-colored eggs.

The hate in their eyes...

We'd raise them from tiny peeping fluffkins, to furious sharp-beaked monsters with otherworldly screeches!

Peep! peep!

Like many first-time chicken farmers, my mother was duped into an excess of roosters, which made the coop particularly violent and scary.

SKREE!

CAW!

Eep!

We'd have to gently boot the roosters off the hens before they completely savaged them to death!

SHOVE

They'd also fight one another!

And more than just chicken-on-chicken casualties—there were also regular break-ins involving various stealthy chicken-killers.

Fox

Weasel

Coyote

Raccoon

Almost every morning, I'd be confronted with some new brutal chicken massacre, which was a bit too much for my tender city-kid sensibilities. I'm still uncomfortable around chickens.

NO RACCOONS FOXES WEASELS OR COYOTES

Eventually, my mom and I weeded down the rooster population by giving them to unsuspecting neighbors. The hens—formerly a terrorized and downtrodden lot— expressed their gratitude by laying TONS of eggs!

Mom tried to keep up with the steady egg supply, making omelets and scrambled eggs, huevos rancheros, fluffy strada, quiche, and homemade mayo.

When she had exhausted her savory egg dish repertoire, she went into a baking frenzy, churning out sweets as fast as the hens could lay.

I perched opportunistically at her elbow as she worked, which was a perfect spot for me to reap the benefits of a sticky spatula or unscraped batter bowl.

Macaroons

Flourless cake

Gingersnaps

Dulce de leche

She began to bake enormous oatmeal raisin cookies and spicy, brittle molasses cookies for the local art movie house to sell at their concessions (she still does this).

She favors buttery pecan-shortbread cookies and powdery almond Russian wedding balls.

I loove these.

I wanted good ol' chocolate chip, which bored her, so I was informed: if I wanted them, I had to learn to make them myself.

So at the start of my independence in the kitchen, I learned the fine art of chocolate chip cookies.

I changed schools a lot— as the new kid, I was always settling in around the fringes. Normally, I would disconnect, burying my nose in a comic book.

But baking became my way to engage while disengaging.

It was a comforting ritual to occupy my nervous energy and fill my belly. Nicely independent and satisfyingly dangerous.

Providing homemade cookies to my classmates was also a good icebreaker at new schools.

Ooh, the oven! Too cool.

I've since turned to the mixing bowl so often in times of turmoil, I can practically bake blindfolded. The act is so soothing—reminding me that I might be a mess, but I can at least do ONE thing right.

COMFORT & TRADITION

I've made:

Almond and chocolate chip

Cakey bourbon balls studded with chocolate bits

Vegan versions, with carob chips and maple syrup

Gingery nutmeg cookies with bittersweet chocolate squares

chocolate-chunk with peanut butter chips

Flattened cinnamon crispies with chocolate centers

Cocoa chocolate chip, with dark rich 97% chocolate

Squishy miniature chocolate chips for road trip snacks

Big bready chocolate chip scones with honey

Delicate tea cookies with lacy edges

Butterscotch chocolate-chunk

Crumbly nutty cookies with a dusting of powdered sugar

For me, the act of assembling and combining chocolate chip cookie ingredients is like watching "The Sound of Music."

Mom might make fun of me for being generic or clichéd in my cookie/movie choices, but when I'm upset, it's all I want.

Lucy— A chicken died—could you clean the coop? xo Mom

The SOUND of MUSIC

♪ I must've had a wicked childhoooood... ♫

(For this to work, it has to be turned off before the Nazi part.)

Cookies

are all about Comfort

Sometimes something simple can comfort the most.

My mother might scoff at the unimaginative chocolate chip cookie, but when she can be persuaded, she makes a mean batch.

After all these years of me ritualistically dropping spoonfuls of chip-peppered dough on baking sheets, she still trumps me in cookie skills.

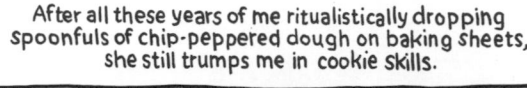

Maybe because baking, unlike cooking, is more of an exact science.

My mother's steady hand and cool head make her an excellent baker, though she prefers the creative freedom of cooking.

My baking is too emotional, too volatile with distress, to ever match Mom's cookie perfection.

But my cookies contain the anxious deliciousness earned through an afternoon spent in turmoil, soothed by separating my troubles into warm crispy pieces.

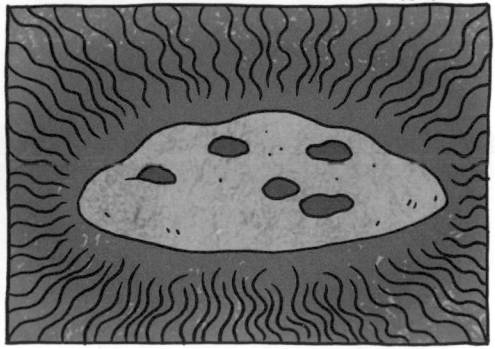

THE BEST CHOCOLATE CHIP COOKIES

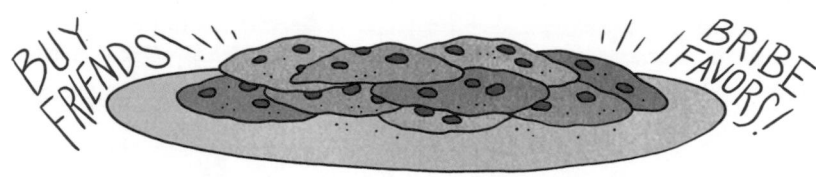

BUY FRIENDS!

BRIBE FAVORS!

YOU'LL NEED

FLOUR
2 CUPS

BAKING SODA 1 TSP

SALT 2 TSP

BUTTER (melted but not hot) 1 CUP

VANILLA 1 Tbsp

CHOCOLATE CHIPS! 12 OZ

SUGAR 3/4 CUP

BROWN SUGAR 3/4 CUP (PACKED)

2 EGGS

COCONUT FLAKES 1 CUP

CHAPTER 4

Thinking back to the foods from our childhoods, my generation reminisces on the culinary delights of well-preserved products of modern science.

I was unaware of these culinary miracles until well after my classmates.

Eating homemade tomato soup for lunch

As a result, something about their foreign-ness has always carried an illicit appeal for me.

Of course, that's not the only reason I like junk food.

It's also DELICIOUS.

People underestimate it, and as much as my parents might keel over to hear me defend it, I find that I often do anyway.

Ugh.

You're just jealous.

On a regular basis, my body craves salts and fats, and there's nothing to be done about it.

Like it or not, human beings have evolved to delight in sugary, fatty, salty deliciousness.

Most of us seem to have problems with moderation, but junk food shouldn't be written off entirely!

As someone who was taught from birth to appreciate the pleasure of eating, I find it discriminatory to dismiss a type of food simply because it's considered unhealthy and cheap.

After all, some of the finest gourmet foods are terribly unhealthy.

I grew up in a household where many of the meals were prepared by my caterer mother.

No, we do not have any *KETCHUP*. I never want to hear that word *AGAIN!*

We ate out often, and most of what I consumed was considered, by adult standards, to be "above standard cuisine."

This is good, Mom, what is it?

Squid.

My parents recall their own childhood dinner tables with shudders.

Frozen fish sticks
TV DINNERS
Jello with carrots
creamed corn
Olive Loaf
Boiled hot dogs
Margarine
Sanka

They grew up to discover food outside the realm of the American standards they had grown up with, and renounced the processed foods from their pasts. They resolved to shield their only daughter from such things.

CHOCO BITS
CHOCO BITS

Denied the grocery favorites of my classmates, junky foods became objects of curiosity and enticement to me, and my most parentally-abhorred form of rebellion.

My discovery of Lucky Charms remains a particularly fond memory.

My middle-school classmate Joe had a mom who didn't cook. She kept her pantry stocked with foods that her adolescent son could prepare.

Among these items was an array of the sugariest, most artificially flavored cereals I'd ever seen.

It was at Joe's house that I discovered:

My parents probably would have intervened if they had known what I was getting into over at Joe's. Somehow, I knew not to mention it to them.

Especially not to my dad...

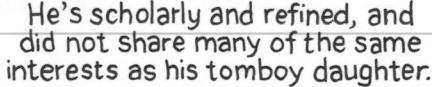

My father has always been torn between wishing me to remain a little girl, and impatiently waiting for me to be old enough to share his interests.

He's scholarly and refined, and did not share many of the same interests as his tomboy daughter.

He couldn't understand why his four-year-old daughter was dead set against a sushi dinner...

...And was baffled when a wine bar didn't allow his five-year old daughter to accompany him for a drink after the opera.

My dad was especially horrified when he took me, as an adolescent, to Rome for spring vacation, and our beautiful hotel on the Piazza del Pantheon was marred by it's proximity to a McDonald's restaurant.

The divorce had been hard on us. While I grew closer with my mom, my dad and I often only saw one another during school vacations. To find common ground, we traveled.

Unfortunately, by the time we went to Rome, I'd been caught up in pre-teen angst, and saw the trip as stealing me away from my friends.

We fought.

The truth is, my dad and I are some-times too similar—too finicky and stubborn and easily wounded—to get along all the time.

Unwilling to sacrifice his vacation to my moods, my dad force-marched me through all the ancient ruins, and wrestled me into every stone-cellar bistro he could find.

He would order osso buco (the tomato-y veal stew) and I would plow through mountains of creamy pasta carbonara.

But despite our Italian favorites, by the end of the week we had argued and sniped at each other to the end of our patience. He left me, sullen and whiny, at the hotel one night to go out on the town.

Scared and angry, I ventured out into the foreign crowd alone, at midnight.

I went to a bar.

I ordered a cup of hot chocolate... ...and was given the most decadent cup of thick, dark chocolate.

When I got back to the hotel, my dad was still out. He didn't return for a few hours, and I was sure he was going to leave me in the hotel forever.

The next day, I left the hotel early.

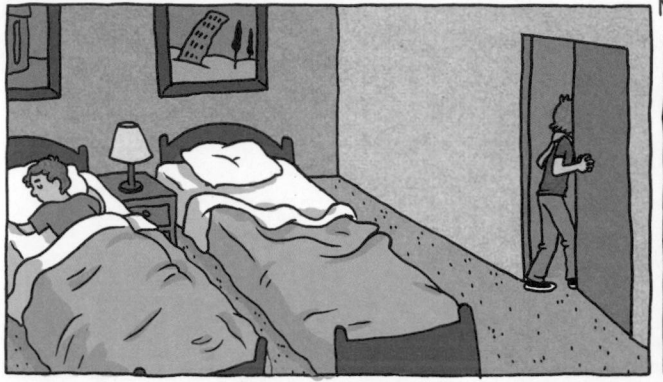

I went straight to the McDonald's in the square.

Even though it was early, I could buy a burger and fries, warm and familiar, the grease eating through the bag, and the smell exactly the same as it was at home.

I sat on the floor of the hotel room, eating my breakfast.

When my dad woke up, the first thing he noticed was what I was eating. Horrified, he berated me for eating junk in one of the finest culinary cities in the world.

HOW CAN YOU DO THAT?!

With relish.

Below us in the piazza, cafes were serving incredible breakfast delicacies.

But I went on, gleefully licking my lips of the salt from the fries, crunching into the familiar, thin-sliced pickle, yellow mustard running down my chin.

When I got home, my mother, having heard about my rebellious breakfast, began a smear campaign to convince me that the hamburgers at McDonald's were actually made of worm meat. Miraculously, I was undeterred.

I remain undeterred to this day. It's not often, but every once in a while, I need those fries.

Oh, nothing, Mom. I'm just eating some, uh... toast.

Ketchup!

She must never know.

Their food has no nutritional value!

I KNOW!

Okay!

More than once I've found myself lost in a foriegn country, when those glowing arches are a welcome sight...

McDonald's

Desperate for a public bathroom

Say what you will...

They've fattened our country to a national obesity crisis!

I know!

We wouldn't be eating it if it didn't taste good.

...A reminder that, despite our cultural differences, we all sometimes need a little comfort grease.

Like everyone, my food pyramid consists of many diverse compartments.

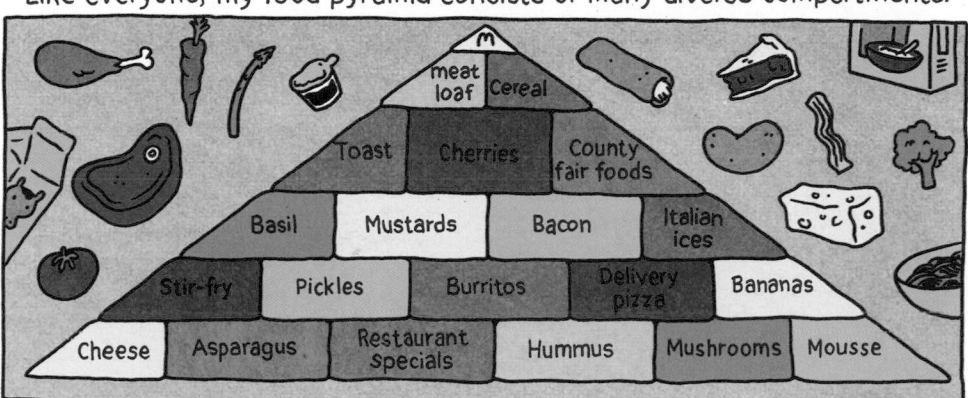

It might not be healthy all the time, and it might not be what my parents wanted for me, but I think I've reached a pretty fair equilibrium for a twenty-something artist.

In my opinion, my parents are missing out.

Anyone who can fail to rejoice in the enticing squish/crunch of a fast-food French fry, or the delight of a warmed piece of grocery-store donut, is living half a life.

CARBONARA

1/2 Lb PANCETTA
(OR THICK-CUT BACON)

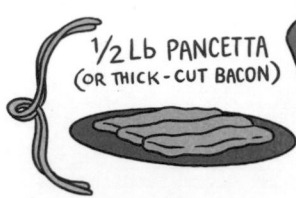

4 CLOVES GAROOOOLIC

OLIVE OIL

BUTTER
1 Tbsp

2 Tbsp

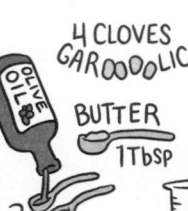

1/4 CUP WHITE WINE

1 Lb SPAGHETTI

3 EGGS
ROMANO   PARMESAN
1/4 CUP   1/2 CUP

2 Tbsp CHOPPED PARSLEY

PUT H_2O ON TO BOIL

(FOR THE SPAGHETTI)

ADD SOME SALT

CUT PANCETTA INTO PIECES ABOUT THE SIZE OF A DIME.

COOK GARLIC IN OIL AND BUTTER 'TILL GOLDEN.

THEN "DISCARD" CLOVES (OR *EAT THEM ON TOAST!*).

COOK THE PANCETTA IN THE HOT, GARLICKY OIL/BUTTER.

ONCE THE PANCETTA IS COOKED, ADD THE WINE.

AN ABSOLUTELY WONDERFUL SMELL!

TRY TO CONTROL YOUR DROOL LONG ENOUGH TO REDUCE THE MIXTURE FOR ABOUT 2 MIN.

ADD SPAGHETTI TO BOILING WATER AND COOK UNTIL TENDER BUT FIRM.

TRY NOT TO EAT ALL OF THE PANCETTA OUTTA THE PAN.

JUST TRY.

BREAK EGGS INTO A BOWL.

SCRAMBLE WITH PARSLEY, PEPPER, AND BOTH CHEESES.

A BIG BOWL!

A FORK MAKES A GOOD SCRAMBLER.

AND EASIER TO CLEAN THAN A WHISK. HA!

ADD HOT DRAINED PASTA TO THE EGG MIX AND STIR IT UP.

THE HEAT FROM THE PASTA WILL COOK THE EGG AND BIND THE NOODLES WITH THE CHEESE, PARSLEY, AND PEPPER.

NOTE: MAKE SURE IF YOU'RE USING BACON, DON'T ACCIDENTALLY BUY "Maple Flavored." THE RESULTS ARE NOT PRETTY.

STIR ME UNTIL THE NOODLES ARE COATED.

PRO TIP: I LIKE TO ADD PEAS (ABOUT A CUP, FRESH OR FROZEN) FOR EXTRA SWEETNESS AND GREEN.

STIR IN THE PANCETTA and SERVE.

SERVES ABOUT 4 (or one)

53

CHAPTER 5

GETTING OURS

There was a time when, preparing for long-distance travel, my top priority was to ensure that I had enough Pixy Stix to last the trip.

To make double sure my supplies lasted, I bought a one-hundred pack of the colorful sugar straws.

Three bucks

For Drew, this bounty was taken as a challenge: finish the bag before we hit Mexico.

By the time we changed planes in Florida, Drew and I were vibrating with sugar.

Four at a time!

Five!

Drew's mother (Betsy) and my own were pals from when they went to boarding school in the seventies.

1972

Their trip to Mexico was meant to be a girly fun-fest, for Mom to recover from her divorce finalizations.

This, I imagine, was expected to be much-hampered by the three children trailing behind.

DEPARTU

Betsy's son, Drew, was born a day after I was.

We've always been very close, since he learned to walk while using my head to steady himself.

Aww...

I'll note that I learned to walk later, as I was smart enough to catch on that they'd carry me if I refused to exert myself.

The year of our Mexico trip, we were twelve and I was still years off from being distinguishable from boys my age.

Sigh.

Drew's little sister, Mason, at eight years (quite a lady)

To avoid the crowded coasts, we were staying in an arty little town, smack in the middle of Mexico.

Mexico

San Miguel

We arrived at our hotel, which was complete with a courtyard of orange trees and secret adobe hiding spots.

We thoroughly explored it from top to bottom (still fueled by colored sugar).

When we got to the room, though, our mothers were snoozing in the twin beds before they could knock back their first round of margaritas.

They were completely bulldozed by the flu within the first few hours of vacation, and spent the next four days in bed, bemoaning their bad luck.

Groaan...

Whiiine...

No T.V, 'cause they chose "quaint"

Left to fend for ourselves, we loitered in the hotel kitchens for a while. The chef's huevos rancheros more than made up for the fact that the hotel didn't have television.

Fresh eggs over black beans, tortilla and salsa verde

The kind hotel chef, Marta

After about an hour, it was clear that we were best kept away from the breakables if we were going to insist on consuming pure sugar in tubes for eight hours straight. We were given a handful of pesos each and ushered feebly out of the hotel.

Moaan.

Scram.

When I think back to this, I recall the exhilaration and disbelief at our good fortune. Here we were, in a new place, pockets full of cash and no parental impositions, set loose in Mexico to do as we pleased.

I remember the feeling of bliss, as we made a beeline toward the center of town, our sneakers pounding up clouds of dust behind us.

I remember all this, and yet, when I think of it, I can't help but wonder:
What were our mothers thinking?

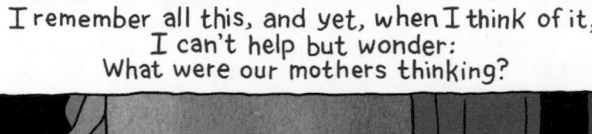

They must have been desperate to risk sending their children off, alone in a strange Mexican town.

Me now

Look, there're stalls up ahead!

Sigh. Ughh.

can too
can not
can not
can too
can too

We must have been *really* annoying.

San Miguel de Allende is small and quirky, but laid out before us, it was a city of unfathomable, undiscovered adventure and excitement.

Adobe buildings flank winding cobble-stone streets, where men sit outside smoking fragrant tabacco.

Food is everywhere — giant strings of dried red peppers hang heavy, rattling in the breeze.

Within the buildings, we discovered an array of tiny shops that smelled, gloriously, of lime and corn tortillas.

There, I ate the best tamales I have ever tasted.

I know they were the best, because we tried as many of the shops as we could find, before we decided on the best one.

Pushcarts peddled sweet corn on a stick, with hot sauce and lime, which turned the corners of our mouths red.

Spicy!

We ate them while sitting on the dusty curb, with cold grapefruit soda, making a mess of our clothes and faces.

The town square hosted a magnificent market-place, where we spent most of our time.

Huge portions of the market were devoted to candy and toy stands.

The toys were fairly boring; mostly plastic tourist fare.

But the candy was both alluring and dangerous. We bought it by the sack, experiencing new revolutions in our sugar-hungry American mouths.

Noise-maker

Lucha libre dude

Keychain that was later taken at customs

Awesome!

There were delicious ones...

...And there were awful ones, that provoked gagging and hilarious laughter.

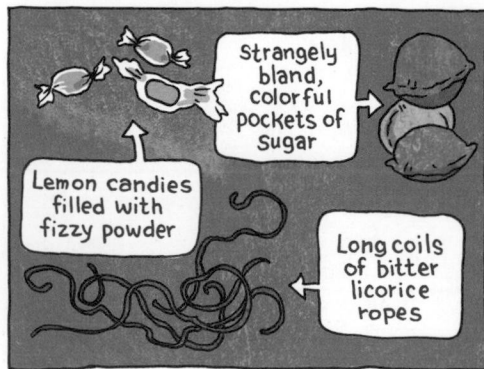

Strangely bland, colorful pockets of sugar

Lemon candies filled with fizzy powder

Long coils of bitter licorice ropes

Sugared, dried, hot pepper candies

Candied cactus

Salty licorice bars

The locals were kind enough to endure us — two sugar-wild and unaccompanied kids, with very little ability to speak and understand Spanish, other than "How much?"

It was the second day of exploration when we discovered the side alley, and the stand where Drew would soon spend a small fortune in pesos.

Quanto questo?

Cactus Candy

Standing before the rack of glossy magazines, I was pensively licking at a spicy, indefinable lollipop when I saw Drew's face go slack with wonder.

Displayed on the rack, without any attempt at concealment, were fifty or so colorful pornographic magazines.

We'd only known American magazine stands, where the pornography was guarded jealously by adults, and our presence near to those rows of black-bagged mysteries was met with rebuke. So we approached cautiously.

To our surprise, the proprietor only pulled a magazine from the rack, and offered it, shining and crisp, into Drew's shaking hands.

Over the next few days, while our mothers languished at the hotel, Drew consumed these magazines in staggering numbers.

Objects from his backpack were discarded; Mad Libs and school reading assignments and a travel Battleship game, displaced to make room for the porn stash. I watched his shoulders begin to strain against the increasing weight of his obsession.

While exploring, we discovered the door to the hotel roof, where he would pore over the magazines, and I would eat candy and occasionally peer over his shoulder, to wrinkle my nose or giggle.

One day, while Drew perused "Mamacita," I stared over the adobe roofs, eating hot candied orange peel, and feeling a little ill.

I worried I was becoming sick, like our mothers had. I was almost right, but I didn't have the flu.

Lookit! Weird, huh?

Eew.

Blood!

Uhhck!

Gross.

Many women recall the flushed embarrassment of purchasing sanitary napkins for the first time, accompanied by Mom as a brand advisor.

Her special day!

I cannot fully recall my feelings, though, buying them alone, from a Mexican druggist who had no idea what I was trying to ask for.

Um.

Hygenicos?

¿Que?

It was bad enough that I had to explain things to Drew...

...But at least now I, too, had something to sneak around in my backpack.

Cram Cram

Sigh.

After our mothers recovered, we spent the rest of the trip sightseeing, driving out to see ancient cliff dwellings, and visiting a hot spring.

We ate in nice restaurants. The food was delicious, but it couldn't quite compare to the cheap food we had discovered in our explorations through town.

Over our meals, I hugged my stomach and drank limonadas (delicious lime, sugar, and sparkling water drinks), while Drew jealously guarded the knapsack he refused to remove at all times, which weighed easily twenty pounds by then.

More recently, we were discussing our time in Mexico while Drew and I were participating in our ritual of tandem cooking.

We often get together to cook meals and discuss old times. Our mothers like to watch us and interject their own perspective on what happened back then.

It was in this way that we learned how Drew had been so effortlessly duped.

What amuses our mothers most, when they tell the story of our Mexican "concurrent coming of age," is that the two of us believed, sincerely, that our secrets were well kept from them.

Our real transition out of childhood was learning of the eternal inability to hide anything from a mom.

They thought they were so mysterious!

HA HA HA HAHAHAA!

In the security line at the Mexican airport, on our way home from our trip, Drew was practically bent double with the weight of his backpack. Our mothers chatted casually to one another about the idiosyncrasies of Mexican airport security.

I heard that the punishments here are severe for anyone trying to smuggle things into the U.S.

Oh yes!

URIDAD URITY

COLORING

Yes, that's right. You could go straight to a Mexican prison, without a trial.

And there are no laws that protect minors.

You know what I heard they hate even more than drug smuggling? Underage kids buying pornography here in Mexico. When they discover it at the border...

Boy, you do NOT want to know what they do!

Cavity searches? Torture? Imprisonment?

That's just the half of it.

COLORING

They have a special smut detector, like a metal detector, but for porn!

hmph giggle

How awful!

DAD

I'm just glad I'm not taking any porno mags in my carry-on. I wouldn't want to go to Mexican prison.

COLORING

When he returned, his backpack was flat and empty, but his back was no straighter.

At least $200 worth of pornographic magazines were now stashed hastily behind a toilet in the men's public bathroom; a treasure for some unsuspecting janitor to discover.

Drew made it through customs without being hauled to Mexican prison, and we returned to America a little more mature.

He missed his souvenirs, but perhaps those kinds of riches are better in moderation.

We've gotten plenty of enjoyment recounting the story over the years.

We agree, there's a feeling about that trip; there was more to it than we knew.

But I guess it's bound to feel a little odd when you accidentally leave something behind in a foreign country.

HUEVOS

THIS IS ONE OF THOSE MEALS THAT YOU HAVE TO MULTITASK, BUT IT MAKES A <u>GREAT</u> MORNING-AFTER MEAL (FOR SUNDAYS OR NEW YEARS DAY).

① YOU'LL NEED:

EGGS TORTILLAS (CORN)

BLACK BEANS SOUR CREAM SALSA CHEESE AVOCADOS

CORN OIL

② GET OIL IN A PAN AND GET IT HOT! FRY BOTH SIDES OF 2 TORTILLAS, JUST UNTIL THEY START TO PUFF (10 SEC)

THEN DRY THEM ON PAPER TOWELS.

③ FRY 1 OR 2 EGGS IN THE REMAINING OIL TO YOUR LIKING, BUT RUNNY IS GOOD. IT SEEPS DOWN INTO THE OTHER LAYERS!

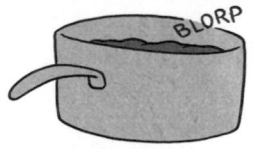

④ WHILE EGGS ARE FRYING, HEAT BEANS ON THE STOVE OR IN THE MICROWAVE.

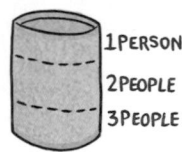

BLORP

1 PERSON
2 PEOPLE
3 PEOPLE

⑤ CUT UP AVOCADOS AND GRATE CHEESE (I LIKE CHEDDAR OR QUESO FRESCO).

⑥ REMOVE BEANS AND EGGS FROM HEAT.

EGG PAPER TOWEL

(TO DE-OIL) TORTILLA

⑦ POUR SALSA OVER BEANS & TORTILLA. (I LIKE SALSA VERDE, BUT YOUR CALL.)

HOT SAUCE

SALSA

VERD

⑧ COMBINE OTHER LAYER INGREDIENTS,

AND EAT.

<u>LAYER DETAILS</u> ⟶

RANCHEROS

(EXPLODED VIEW)

THE STRATA

CHEESE

SALSA

EGG/S

TORTILLA

SOUR CREAM

AVOCADO

SALSA

BEANS

TORTILLA

(LAYERS CAN BE REPEATED AS NECESSARY)

CHAPTER 6

THE CRAVER

When I was little, my mother would often make me enormous plates of sautéed mushrooms in garlic.

I wasn't a picky eater, I was exactly the opposite. I would try almost anything, and almost always found it to be delicious.

What are you eating?

Pickle sandwich.

Still one of my favorites.

But I was a *craver*.

Can we have yams?

Yams?

Please?

I craved the crispy chicken skin, salty and crackling, and would pick it from the chicken dinner while her back was turned.

Frequently, there were already frayed edges around the chicken that were barely noticeable.

Heyyy...

What?

My mother, fastidious about her professional cooking, had fewer scruples about the family dinner, and the sanctity of the chicken skin.

Never let your fingers accidentally touch the food.

FLOUR

Once we discovered our mutual illicit appreciation, my father was hopelessly outnumbered.

Why do we never have any skin on our chicken?

Typical breakfast foods didn't appeal, so in the mornings, I craved Mexican food.

For years I ate rice and beans for breakfast.

Always reading at the table.

It wasn't that my mother was overindulgent. I was never allowed sugar cereal, or given cheetos dinners.

Lunch?

She found it endearing, and she sympathized, because she, herself, is a craver.

Whatcha making?

Russian wedding cookies.

Why?

I really want one!

Like me, my mother has frequent cravings for red meat.

Very hot, black cast iron pan

Sizzle sizzle

When I was a teenager, when she wasn't with my vegetarian stepfather, she would make enormous steaks, and we would eat them rare off the cutting board.

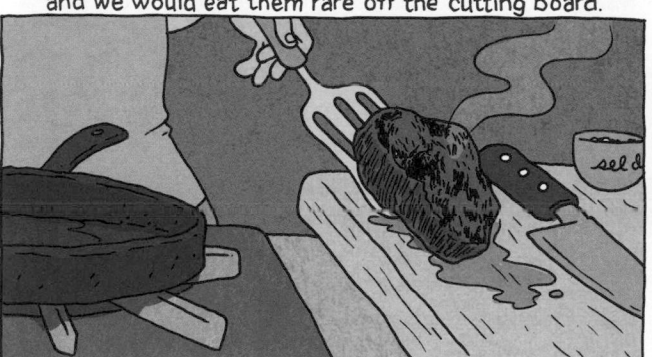

sel d

We could barely wait for them to repose, soaking in their juices and still sizzling a little from the skillet.

Reposing helps to flavor and soften the meat.

It was a little witchy; two females, standing, cutting into a salty, bloody hunk of meat—the juice running down our chins.

We'd run our fingers through the juice and lick our lips and moan.

Sometimes we'd sauté spinach. We'd throw wet handfuls into a giant pot with olive oil and garlic until it was limp and dark.

Then we'd eat just that, in enormous bowls, for dinner.

Watching "Antonia's Line"

When we gardened, I would catch her biting into a warm, freshly husked tomatillo, the green flesh crunching quietly.

I preferred the sweet, dusty, red cherry tomatoes.

But eventually, tomatillos became my favorites, too.

A woman's body craves protein and iron.

I grew into my mother's cravings—the demands of my inherited body chemistry.

How many of my cravings are learned behavior, versus the uncontrollable inherited needs of my cells?

How much of a difference is there, really, between genetics and the legacy of my nutritional history?

I wonder this when considering how, before I even asked, she would set before me a plate of sautéed mushrooms, cooked with salt and garlic and olive oil, a strange and eccentric meal, and exactly what I'd been craving.

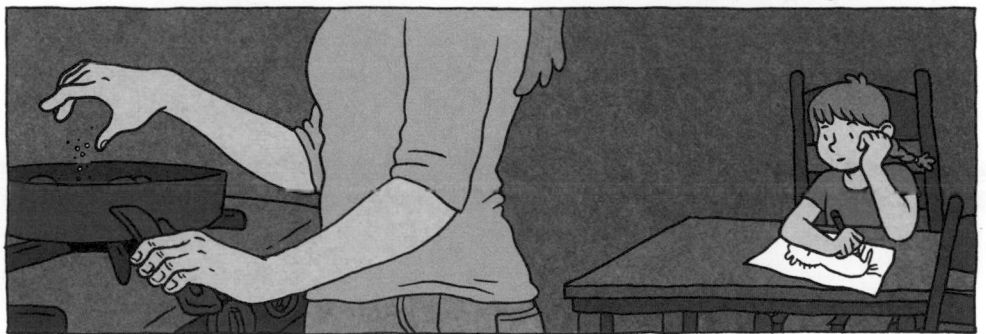

The Way Mom Makes Mushrooms

Watch this!

Only lost one!

HOW DOES SHE DO THAT!?

MOM IS A DEVOTED FOLLOWER OF THE WONDERFUL JULIA CHILD, SO HER MUSHROOM TECHNIQUE OWES MUCH TO MISS JULIA.

THEY EVEN MET ONCE

I LOVE YOU.

?

FIRST OF ALL, GET THE BIGGEST PAN YOU HAVE.

IF YOU DON'T HAVE ONE, DO IT IN BATCHES OR IN TWO SMALL PANS AT ONCE.

 ## ALSO GET:

A SPATULA

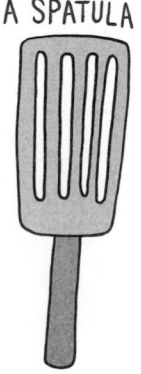

A DISH TOWEL

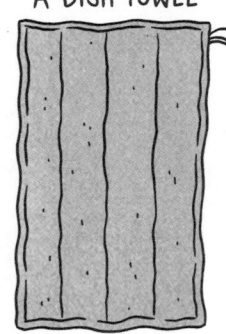

A BIG PLATE

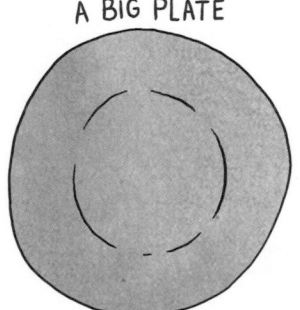

A GLASS OF SOMETHING NICE TO DRINK

BUYING MUSHROOMS

AT GROCERY STORES YOU'LL LIKELY FIND *WHITE MUSHROOMS* AKA: BUTTON, BABY BELLA, OR CREMINI.*

* THESE ARE SLIGHTLY DIFFERENT, BUT PRETTY SIMILAR.

BUT AT FARMERS MARKETS... YOU'LL FIND TYPES LIKE

PORTOBELLO   MORELS   CHANTERELLES

OR MY FAVORITES: *Shiitakes*

YOU NEVER WANT TO WASH MUSHROOMS. THEY'RE LIKE LITTLE SPONGES, SO THEY SOAK UP WATER AND GET SOGGY (gross).

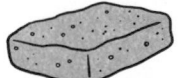

=

IF THEY'RE REALLY DIRTY, JUST PAT THEM (LIGHTLY) WITH A DAMP CLOTH AND THEN LET THEM DRY FOR A BIT.

SOGGINESS AWAY!

I DON'T ALWAYS CLEAN FARMERS MARKET MUSHROOMS, 'CAUSE I DON'T MIND A BIT OF DIRT.

HMM

BUT *DO* CHECK FOR BUGS!

SERIOUSLY THOUGH

LET 'EM DRY.

THIS WILL BE IMPORTANT TO MAKE THEM SAUTÉ RIGHT.

COMBINE SOME BUTTER *
AND OLIVE OIL IN YOUR PAN.
(JULIA RECOMMENDS 1 PART
OLIVE OIL TO 2 PARTS BUTTER.)
ADD ENOUGH TO SHINE THE
WHOLE PAN BOTTOM.

OLIVE OIL

*JUST OIL IS OKAY,
TOO, FOR
VEGANS.

BUTTER

TURN YOUR
STOVE ON **HOT**.

SIZZLE

WAIT UNTIL THE
BUTTER STOPS FOAMING
AND THE PAN IS *REALLY HOT*.

BRING IT ON!

SIZZLE

SOME PEOPLE LIKE TO CUT OFF
THE MUSHROOM STEMS, BUT
MOM USUALLY DOESN'T. THE
STEMS ARE GOOD! BUT TRIM
OFF THE HARD BITS BEFORE
ADDING THE MUSHROOMS
TO THE PAN.

DUMP

TURN DOWN
THE HEAT TO
MEDIUM

NOW THIS IS IMPORTANT

BE SURE YOU ALLOW PLENTY OF SPACE IN THE PAN FOR THEM!
IF YOU CROWD THE MUSHROOMS, THEY'LL STEAM UNEVENLY
—THEY WON'T SAUTÉ AND BECOME BROWN AND CRISPY.

YES

NO

NOW LET THEM BE FOR A WHILE. THEY'LL SOAK UP THE OILS AND THE PAN WILL GET DRY AND THEN THEY'LL START TO

THIS IS A GOOD SIGN! DON'T ADD MORE OIL/BUTTER, EVEN IF THEY START TO SMOKE A LITTLE — JUST TURN DOWN THE HEAT AND WATCH THE MUSHROOMS START TO SWEAT.

SQUEEEAK!

PHEW!

WHEN THEY START TO BROWN, STIR AND SHAKE.

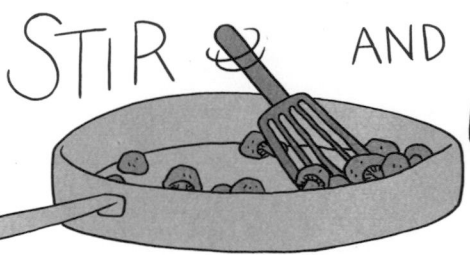

DISHTOWEL →

WHEN THEY SEEM BROWN AND CRISPY AND STILL MOIST, PUT THEM ON A PLATE AND ADD SALT AND PEPPER!

BEST EATEN WITH YOUR HANDS!

CHAPTER 7

ON
FOREIGN
SOY

No place has ever made me feel as foreign as Tokyo.

My boy haircut when I was 14

EXTREMELY jet-lagged.

Shibuya girl

Not least due to the fact that I am allergic to soy, which seemed to be in everything!

SOY POPS

Soy noodles

Soy tea

Soy Paste

I had to be careful about what I ate.

SOY DUMPLINGS

I was almost always hungry.

Soy SOUP

SOYBEANS

SOY CANDY

When I was fourteen, my friend Drew moved to Japan with his family. I spent a week visiting him soon after they settled.

What does "gaijin" mean?

"White tourist."

Gaijin!

ha

Searching for non-soy foods, I came upon sweet, soft, comforting mochi, which I devoured.

(Bready bean-paste dumplings)

When you eat sushi, you should eat the whole piece in one bite, unless you want to make a big mess.

Aargh ooo rugh?

* Are you sure?

Expert

Learning

Whiskey & cigars

Drew was eager to show me all the illicit goodies available to underage kids in Tokyo —

He favored contraband that reminded him of home back in the states.

Sushi moving by on a conveyer belt!

Eating and buying food was always an adventure into a completely new realm of tastes and cultural imagery.

Shiokara

Do these things have addictive drugs in them?

Ten at a time

POCKY

Sweet and salty squid candies

The candy store near Drew's apartment was almost blinding in its array of intriguing neon goodies, marketed by strange and colorful characters.

Panty vending machine!

Wow.

Cool!

This one's got a cartoon eel on it!

It was nice to be among people who recognized the power of cartoons.

EAT.

BUY.

Anpanman, who has a head that is a giant bean cake.

89

91

Because my mother was hungry for a glimpse of ancient Japan (and she was going broke in expensive Tokyo), we headed out of the city.

In a serenity garden, in a little Soji-screen house, we had a traditional, many-course meal...

Salty dried fish with the heads on

warm sake

Gyoza dumplings with shrimp

Squid with dark sauce

Sweet eel soup

Fish cakes

Sashimi

Rice with seaweed

Miso soup

wasabi

yaki-onigiri

Dorayaki— sweet bean cakes

Kabocha squash

Sweet curd in bean paste

Tea

I wasn't used to a meal with so many courses.

It's polite to eat with enthusiasm, but it's difficult to seem thrilled by the eleventh course or so.

Eating soy, even though I know it'll make me sick.

Hey Drew!

Drew went to the American school, so he had other expatriate friends, but I'm sure he still felt isolated at an awkward age.

The American embassy in Tokyo had a bowling alley!

I couldn't imagine starting high school as an American in Japan.

As if being fourteen isn't strange and alienating enough.

Average fourteen-year-old Tokyo boy

Drew, big for his age

At least he wasn't a picky eater.

He adapted very well, actually.

We were visiting during the rainy season in June, when the streets fill with jewel-colored umbrellas.

Arigato gozaimasu!

Do itashi machite.

We waited out the rain indoors, watching Japanese television and practicing our pronunciation.

"Tampopo," Japanese film about food →

Drew lived around the corner from a noodle shop, where we ate ramen soup with noodles, broth, vegetables, egg, and spices...

...Nothing like the salty microwavable ramen I was used to, back home.

Top Ramen
Just add water!

↑
NOT THE SAME
↓

Not to knock Americanized ramen.

It comprised a large portion of my diet through high school.

HOW TO MAKE SUSHI ROLLS

SUSHI IS WAY EASIER TO MAKE THAN IT SEEMS!

IT'S ALSO PRETTY HEALTHY AND _WAY_ CHEAPER TO MAKE THAN TO BUY.

PLUS, IT'S FUN TO DO AND LOOKS IMPRESSIVE WHEN YOU PREPARE IT FOR FRIENDS.

THIS RECIPE IS AN AMERICANIZED VEGGIE VERSION OF MAKI ROLLS.

I MAKE IT A LOT, BECAUSE A CARTOONIST WHO LOVES SUSHI IS SOON A BROKE(R) CARTOONIST.

I USE SWEET POTATOES, AVOCADOS, AND CUCUMBERS...

...BUT IT'LL ALSO WORK GREAT WITH THINGS LIKE RAW TUNA, SAUTÉED MUSHROOMS, SCALLIONS,

OR ANYTHING ELSE YOU LIKE IN SUSHI!

WITH THANKS TO MY ART TEACHER WENDY, WHO FIRST SHOWED ME HOW TO DO THIS!

YOU WILL NEED

UNFURLED? FURLED? WORN AS A HAT

A BAMBOO SUSHI MAT

BOTAN

SUSHI RICE (DON'T JUST USE REGULAR RICE)

SEAWEED SHEETS, OR NORI

NORI

1 SWEET POTATO
1 AVOCADO
1 CUCUMBER

PLUS:

A SHARP KNIFE

PICKLED GINGER *

SOY SAUCE

SESAME SEEDS *

UNAGI SAUCE * (EQUAL PTS. SOY, MIRIN & SUGAR)

FLOUR

WATER

WASABI *

CORN OIL

CHOP-STICKS *

*OPTIONAL

 COOK THE RICE IN A POT OR RICE COOKER
(THIS USUALLY TAKES ABOUT 45 MIN)

YOU CAN MAKE THE RICE STICKIER BY RINSING IT
IN A SIEVE UNDER COLD WATER BEFORE COOKING.

THE WATER-TO-RICE COOKING RATIO WILL BE WRITTEN ON THE BAG.

BOTAN

SO WILL THE TIME IT TAKES FOR YOUR RICE BRAND TO COOK.

ONCE IT'S DONE, **WAIT FOR THE RICE TO COOL!** SERIOUSLY. DO IT.

UGH—BUT I'M HUNGRY NOW!!

TOO BAD.

SO SAD.

MEANWHILE
PEEL & CUT SWEET POTATOES INTO LONG, THIN STRIPS.

CUT, RAW SWEET POTATOES SMELL LIKE FLOWERS!

≀≀≀ HEAT OIL ⟩⟩⟩

ABOUT AN INCH DEEP.

IN A BIG SAUCEPAN

DON'T USE OLIVE OIL FOR FRYING. IT'S MEANT FOR USE AT LOWER TEMPERATURES.

MIX FLOUR AND WATER TO THE CONSISTENCY OF GLUE.

FLOUR = IN A BOWL

TOSS IN THE STRIPS OF SWEET POTATOES AND COAT THEM WITH THE FLOUR MIXTURE.

THEN FRY THE BATTERED SWEET POTATOES IN OIL.

SIZZLE

FRY UNTIL CRISPY

THEN PUT ON THEM A PAPER TOWEL TO SOAK UP THE EXCESS OIL.

CUT THE AVOCADO AND CUCUMBER INTO LONG SKINNY STRIPS.

NOW COMES THE SUSHI-ING!

SETUP

BOWL OF WATER

A DRINK*

VEGGIES

RICE

NORI

SPATULA

KNIFE

BAMBOO MAT

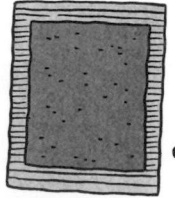

PLACE THE NORI ON THE BAMBOO MAT (SHINY SIDE UP).

SPREAD RICE EVENLY OVER THE NORI IN A ½ INCH LAYER, LEAVING 1½ INCHES AT THE TOP.

LAY VEGGIES ACROSS THE RICE BED.

WET YOUR HANDS IN WATER BOWL AND RUN THEM OVER THE BARE PORTIONS OF THE NORI, WETTING IT SO IT'LL STICK.

*

SUPER DELISH SUSHI DRINK

SELTZER

OVER ICE

GRATE GINGER

MAPLE SYRUP

(TO TASTE)

LIME

AND IF YOU'RE INTO IT → TO TASTE

OR

PIMMS No 1

VODKA

THE NEXT PART TAKES SOME PRACTICE

FLIP UP THE END OF THE MAT CLOSEST TO YOU.

FLIP

SMOOSH THE END OF THE NORI OVER, FOLDING IT ON TO THE RICE.

THEN ROLL BACK THE MAT SO IT DOESN'T GET ROLLED INTO YOUR SUSHI, AND USE IT TO CAREFULLY ROLL YOUR MAKI.

ROLL

(ROLL MAKI, ROLL MAT, SCOOCH THE MAT/MAKI DOWN, REPEAT)

WHEN YOUR ROLL IS ALL ROLLED UP, SQUEEZE IT IN THE MAT (JUST A LITTLE!).

IF THE ROLL IS TOO FAT FOR THE NORI TO CONTAIN, YOU'LL HAVE TO REMOVE SOME OF THE RICE OR VEG.

REMOVE THE BAMBOO MAT AND YOU SHOULD HAVE SOMETHING LIKE THIS:

THEN WET THE BLADE OF YOUR KNIFE WITH WET CLOTH (CAREFUL!).

THE WETTER YOUR KNIFE, THE EASIER IT'LL BE TO CUT THE MAKI.

YOU MAY NEED TO RE-WET.

SLIDE

DON'T JUST CHOP, OR YOU'LL SMOOSH IT!

TA DA!

EAT WITH SOY SAUCE, GINGER, SESAME SEEDS, AND UNAGI SAUCE!

LEFTOVER CUCUMBER WITH RICE VINEGAR & SESAME OIL

CHAPTER 8

The Apple Doesn't Fall

Far from the Cheese

My parents moved to New York City in the late seventies, where they lived the kind of Manhattan life that has since migrated to Brooklyn.

Mom had her new art degree.

Dad was getting into advertising.

They had a small apartment in the Village, and lived cheaply among artists, musicians, and yuppies alike.

My dad entered the business world, and my mom considered her post-college options.

Just out of school, she was curious about the world of food.

Exploring the city one day, she walked into a tiny gourmet food shop called Dean & DeLuca.

Within 20 minutes of entering the store...

It was a demanding job.

...Mom was wearing an apron behind the cheese counter!

But Mom was a natural.

That's not to say that Georgio DeLuca was an easygoing boss...

This is no good! Redo this display!

CHEESE

TOSS

There, behind the counter at D&D, surrounded by towers of stacked Alpine cheeses and smelling of the ripest bries, my mother became master of her charges.

My father, returning home from his job in advertising, would be greeted by my mother's earthy cheese smell — clinging to her hair and skin— which he loved.

Snifff!

Working alongside her were musicans, painters, writers, and students.

It's nice, of course, to have professionals in the kitchen, but it might be said that without creative people from other spheres, restaurants miss out on something...

I love to hear her stories from back then; about the burgeoning edible revolution, the backstage tales of now-famous kitchens.

In present-day Manhattan, this has become rare, as so many trained culinary professionals come to New York to work in food that there are fewer jobs washing dishes or waiting tables to pay the rent for artists or students.

When Mom started out, New York was still building its reputation as a culinary mecca. It was a different city from what it is today.

The other reason I like these stories so much is that this was the time when she became pregnant with me.

She describes how she would haul enormous rounds of Gruyère from the cooler to the case, customers peering at how she perched it on her swollen belly.

Later, she would speculate on how this affected me – how I was imbued with a love of cultured dairy by sheer prenatal proximity.

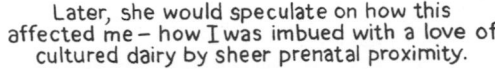

Around that same time, she volunteered at the Whitney Museum...

and manned a table selling produce at the Greenmarket.

Throughout all of it, she painted.

I have to admit, I've thus far managed to support her theories of fetal imprinting.

My first "job," at the age of three or four, was helping my mom at the Greenmarkets, which were starting up all over Manhattan and Brooklyn. As a city kid, I loved the smell of hay and apples, the giant pumpkins, that *seemed* so foreign in my world.

After my parents split up and Mom and I moved upstate to live in the country, I was recruited to help with her new catering company. It had quickly become popular for small gatherings and events hosted by fellow former Manhattanites, or weekenders up from the city.

Mom would occasionally help cater big shoots for Annie Leibovitz, the famed photographer.

She shot a Kate Hudson "Vanity Fair" cover once, in a rainy, muddy field, and I was on hand with the tea and cheese platters.

She lived near our home in upstate New York.

I spent the day slogging back and forth in the mud between the little portable kitchen and the catering tent housing the spare models.

The models, I found, were fun to serve — mostly ignoring the food and hobnobbing.

As the rainy day wore on, I was sent across the field with hot tea for Ms. Hudson, who was being photographed while standing in a frigid stream in the rain wearing a flimsy nightgown.

She was nearly blue with cold, soaked and shivering, standing in water up to her knees.

It's quite a thing for the coffee kid to be completely unjealous of an acclaimed actress, but I can tell you that I wouldn't have switched places with her that day.

I went away grateful for my thick catering jacket, and went back to hide from the rain in the model tent, listening to them flirt and watching them move gracefully on the uneven ground.

Another time, we cooked for an event at the extravagant home of art collectors.

I suppose we should get your chef's jacket cleaned.

gravy

caviar

vinegar

Their enormous house was filled with strange light installations, sculptures, and scores of gorgeous paintings.

Wow!

They also bred poodles.

I had just hoisted a particularly large tray of elegant tea cakes, when I felt a tug on my pant leg.

TUG TUG

Skittering around my feet was a toy poodle that was missing half its face.

Oh my GOD!

Uh...

Woah!

What is that?

Shaking

Nice.. ...doggy.

The poodle, it turns out, was a much-loved pet and breeder dog, and had been treated for jaw cancer at the family's great expense.

It had gone on to look like something out of the Terminator movies.

Nice little dog, though.

Catering isn't particularly steady work, at least not the way Mom did it. She would turn down jobs while she pursued other interests.

When she noticed that many of the local farmers brought their wares all the way down to the city, she helped to organize the farmers market locally in our small town of Rhinebeck.

Making holiday gift baskets for the market

She and I worked as vendors for a local fruit farm.

Peach fuzz gets EVERYWHERE. And ITCHES!

In the winter, I'd work in the farm's country store.

My favorite thing to do at the store was to make the cider doughnuts.

WELCOME

We had this cool old machine that trucked the raw dough into a channel of hot oil (dangerous), then pooped them out onto a tray, where they were coated with grainy sugar. After they cooled, I'd test them for quality.

Dough loop

Spitting hot oil

TA DA!

Sugar

Roll around

Hot, doughy, delicious

In the spring, I would work for a neighbor who grew organic shiitake mushrooms.

Part of my job was to carefully tap each mushroom as I picked it, watching the tiny bugs flee the gills in the underside of the cap.

Then my mother and I would sell the mushrooms for our neighbor at the farmers market in town.

Rhinebeck had always been a pretty quiet town, with a handful of hardware and smoke shops for the upstate locals and the Manhattan weekenders.

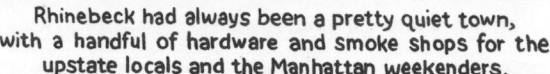

After the Rhinebeck farmers market took off, fresh, local goods could be found close to the farm sources, and the town began to garner new interest from surrounding towns and the city. Its culture and economy grew, developing Rhinebeck into a Hudson Valley art and cultural center, not to mention a foodie hotspot.

At the farmers market, we started selling cheese from a few local artisanal dairies. (The Hudson Valley is home to a lot of gorgeous little organic dairy farms.)

At sixteen, I would drive my rickety clunker all over the Catskill Mountains, stopping at little farms to pick up our order every week.

Nettle Meadow is a gorgeous little goat farm that also ran animal rescue and housing. The cheese was touted as "Happy Goats, Good Cheese!"

Old Chatham is a family-owned sheep farm, and one of the most successful in the Hudson Valley.

But my favorite stop was Sprout Creek Farm, which is run by farmer nuns!

Whenever I stopped by to pick up the cheese, there was always some wonderful honey festival or hot air balloon event – usually some inner-city kids petting a goat, or some investment banker up with his family, learning to milk a cow. Their cheese was some of the best I've ever had.

The last catering event that I worked with my mom before I left for art school was the preopening reception for the DIA Beacon, a modern-art museum on the Hudson River.

Renovated factory space right on the riverbank

The guests milled around in the freshly whitewashed galleries. The sprawling building was still empty of art, save for a few pieces that had been built into the space, and everything echoed in the empty high-ceilinged rooms.

Once the toasts began and the hors d'oeuvres ran out, I slipped away to explore.

With a few minutes reprieve from serving sashimi and mushroom puffs, I wandered around the empty museum, thinking about art.

I was due to pack up and leave for art school in Chicago in the fall, and I was nervous.

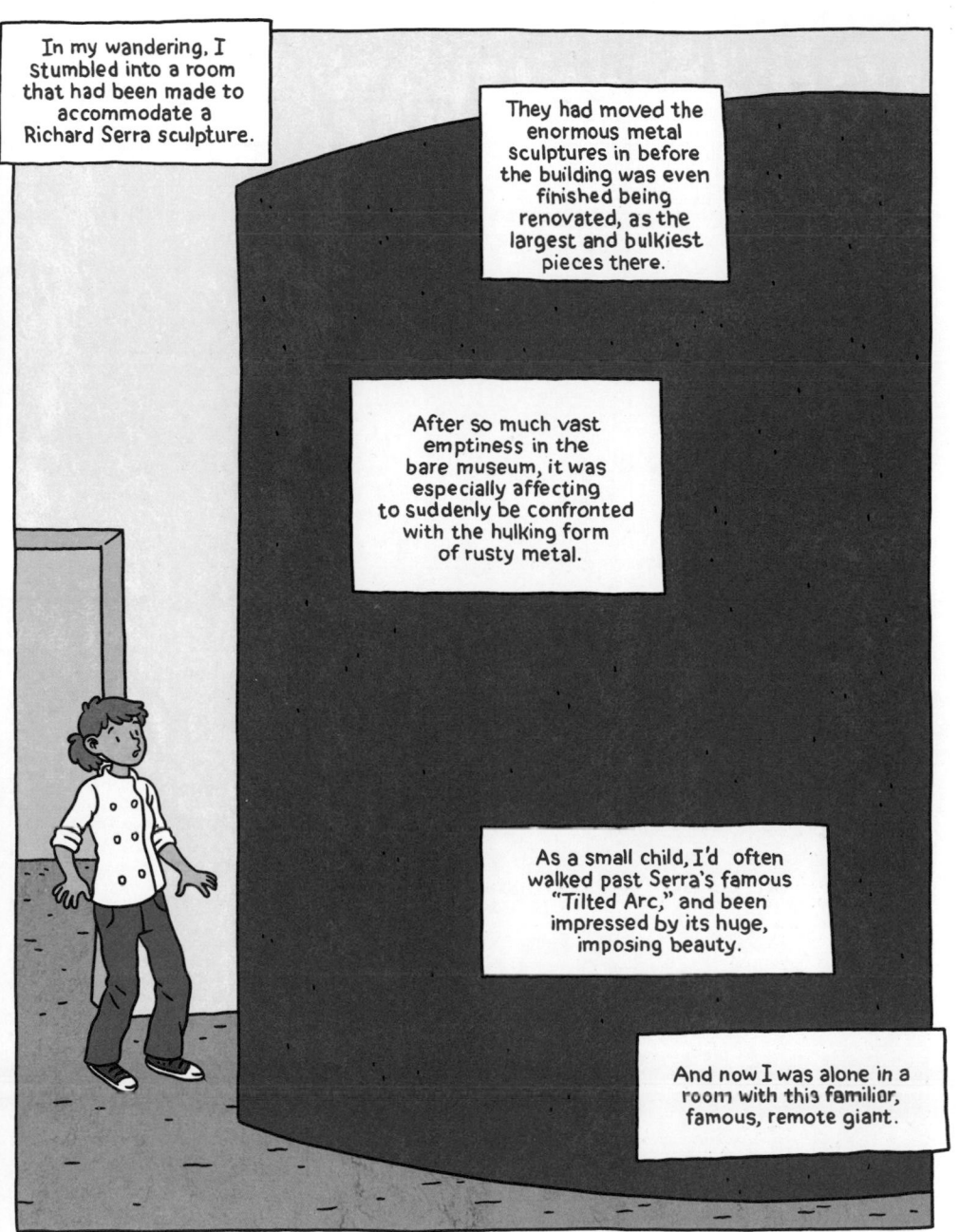

In my wandering, I stumbled into a room that had been made to accommodate a Richard Serra sculpture.

They had moved the enormous metal sculptures in before the building was even finished being renovated, as the largest and bulkiest pieces there.

After so much vast emptiness in the bare museum, it was especially affecting to suddenly be confronted with the hulking form of rusty metal.

As a small child, I'd often walked past Serra's famous "Tilted Arc," and been impressed by its huge, imposing beauty.

And now I was alone in a room with this familiar, famous, remote giant.

There were no guards to shoo me away.

I was free to run my palm over the cool surface— to press my cheek and ear to it and hear the dull echo-y thunk when I knocked against it.

I could be still with this piece of imposing artwork, unobserved and uncrowded.

I was an eighteen-year-old kid in a dirty waitstaff uniform, with tired feet and pre-college jitters.

But I could be alone, touching the cool metal of a famous and affecting work of art,

a gift gained through circumstance.

I thought of all the builders and guards and custodians who have had similar moments, and felt lucky to be a server.

Inspired, I tackled art school with my all.

I was homesick, but I was lucky to have family in Chicago.

I would drag my paint-stained, bedraggled self to their house for Sunday dinners.

Like most of my family, my aunt and uncle are very into cooking, despite having three kids with varying degrees of pickiness.

It was at one of these dinners that my aunt Anne asked if I would help her out with a series of food reviews she'd agreed to do as an extension of her journalism job.

Because you have to try a variety from the menu while writing a review, she needed a hungry mouth to get a wider range of tastes.

And I was available when her professional adult pals were too busy with work.

Anne was sometimes too busy, so occasionally she'd have my friend and me go, instead, and send her our notes.

It was a good time to be an eater in Chicago.

The city had always been a great meat-and-potatoes town, but the culinary scene was becoming more diverse.

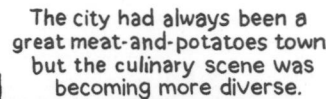

City of Industry and Molecular Gastronomy

Innovative chefs and great new restaurants were arriving in the Midwestern city, and the food scene was growing steadily.

FOOD & DRINK
ALINEA
BLACKBIRD

By the time I graduated, I had learned my way around Chicago as a thriving culinary city of foodie delights.

This used to be a dog groomer!

Now it's a fancy pub!

One of these delights was Fox & Obel.

FOX & OBEL

The gourmet store was founded by two lawyers who loved food, and started F&O with the intention of capitalizing on the culinary gold rush in Chicago

Mr. Fox   Mr. Obel

(I actually have no idea how these gentlemen look.)

It was one of my favorite places in the city— where, surrounded by exotic and delicious smells, I'd be comforted during stressful finals weeks, soothed by the presence of fifty-year-old oak-aged balsamic.

The bottle was $200!

During graduation week, I was feeling nervous about my soon-to-be status as a Bachelor of Fine Arts, so I went to F&O for a comforting chunk of Humboldt Fog goat cheese.

FOX & OBEL

The delicious smell of food that I can't afford

When I looked around, clutching my $6 chèvre, I noticed that I wasn't the only student in the place.

They were behind counters, mopping the floors, and stocking the shelves.

New York might be a closed book for jobs for someone like me, but Chicago was going through its renaissance of food, and there were still opportunities for a kid like me.

I asked for an application while the cashier scanned my cheese, and had an interview within a few days!

APPLICATION

In Mom's day, you could be hired as long as you had the time and inclination.

I had to answer a bunch of psychological questions.

And take a drug test.

Here's your apron.

Which cheese would you bring to a desert island?

talking to Mom

pee cup

It was the seventies when I was a cheese-monger... If they'd had drug tests back then, we'd have been short a whole store staff!

Days later, I was behind the counter in the same sort of starchy monger's jacket my mom had worn 30 years earlier.

It felt natural (and overwhelming) to be there among the hundreds of cheeses, tasting unfamiliar ones and learning to use the cutter and wrapper.

I was working alongside musicians, artists, actors, and students who had finagled jobs there because they, too, loved the fancy food they couldn't afford.

Bernie

Lydia

Mark

Jen

HEES

Nate

Ella

So I transitioned out of college into the "real world" with the comforting taste of Australian feta, crusty English cheddar, and dark, earthy blue.

F&O

(I have to know the cheeses to talk to customers.)

In the name of sales!

My favorite treat was warmed Cantal (a medium-hard French picnic cheese) on crusty bread pilfered from the bakery's day-old rejects.

saran

scorching hot saran-cutting metal bar

warming stone

cheese melting on wax paper

Every day, I would ride my bike to work, past the fragrant chocolate factory that sent clouds of intoxicating melting chocolate smells thick into the air.

Sometimes after work, my boyfriend would come down to the store to pick me up and we'd use my employee discount to take a cheese picnic to the lakeshore while the elation of the summer boiled around us.

In a city that spends so much time being cold and sleety, beautiful summer days are especially sweet and celebrated for their rarity and surprise.

Just like a rare and expensive delicious treat to a poor college kid.

A SECOND-GENERATION CHEERFUL CHEESEMONGER'S
CHEESE CHEAT SHEET

Working as a cheesemonger has taught me a LOT about cheese, but it's still easy to be overwhelmed by the cheese counter.

Dang.

There are just *SO MANY KINDS* of cheese, and every one is different, and it's hard to remember what's good.

CHEESE

SO HERE ARE SOME OF THE THINGS I LEARNED WHILE CHEESEMONGERING!

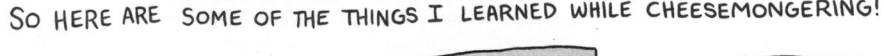

CATEGORIZING CHEESE IS COMPLICATED.

WHO AM I?

WHAT DOES IT MEAN?

THERE'S NO UNIVERSAL CHEESE CATEGORIZATION METHOD— RATHER, THERE ARE LOTS.

TYPE OF MILK IN CHEESE
COW   SHEEP   GOAT   BUFFALO   YAK   ?

RIND TYPE ON CHEESE
BLOOMY   WASHED   WRAPPED   BLUE

CHEESE HARDNESS
SOFT   SEMI-SOFT   MEDIUM HARD   HARD

AGE OF CHEESE
FRESH/NEW   SLIGHTLY AGED   MORE AGED   AGED 10+ YEARS

BUT EVEN MORE SUB-CLASSIFICATIONS EXIST. OH JEEZ, NOW I'M CONFUSING YOU.

FOR EXAMPLE, ONE OF MY FAVORITE CHEESES, <u>CANTAL</u>, CAN BE CATEGORIZED LIKE THIS:

- It's COW'S MILK AND RAW (UNPASTURIZED)
- It's AGED SIX MONTHS TO A YEAR
- It's A CAVE-AGED, CLOTHBOUND RIND CHEESE
- It's SEMI-HARD AND MELTS WELL (GRILLED CHEESE!)

<u>BUT</u> It's <u>ALSO</u> A FRENCH CHEESE, A WINTER CHEESE (THE COWS FED ON HAY, NOT GRASS), AND IT CHANGES COLOR, TEXTURE, AND TASTE AS IT AGES.

SEE WHY THIS IS SO COMPLICATED?

I'M COMPLICATED.

BUT AWESOME.

OK, ENOUGH ABOUT CATEGORIZATION. *WHATEVER.*

SIX TOTALLY AMAZING THINGS I LEARNED ABOUT CHEESE:

ALPINE CHEESES ARE THE ONES THAT COME IN WHEELS, SO THEY CAN BE *ROLLED* DOWN THE MOUNTAINS WHERE THEY'RE MADE.

WHEEEE!

A LOT OF CHEESE ISN'T VEGETARIAN. A CURDLING AGENT KNOWN AS "RENNET" IS MADE FROM ANIMAL PRODUCTS, BUT THERE IS SUCH A THING AS VEGETABLE RENNET.

ONE CHEESE WITH VEGGIE RENNET, PLEASE!

AGING CHEESES BREAKS DOWN LACTOSE, SO MOST AGED CHEESES CAN BE EATEN BY LACTOSE INTOLERANTS!

 GOOD NEWS!

AGING ALSO BREAKS DOWN MOST POTENTIALLY HARMFUL BACTERIA, SO LESS WORRY ABOUT RAW MILK CHEESES!

MOST CHEESE RINDS ARE EDIBLE – YUMMY, EVEN! BUT THEY ARE WHERE YOU'D MOST LIKELY ENCOUNTER LISTERIA OR CHEESE MITES.*

PROVE YOU'RE HARD-CORE... ...EAT MY RIND.

*BUGS USED TO AERATE THE CHEESE.

BLUE CHEESE IS A SPECIAL TYPE OF MOLD THAT CAN ACTUALLY SPREAD TO OTHER CHEESES!

LIKE A ZOMBIE CHEESE!

BUT NOT ALL CHEESES WITH VEINS ARE BLUE.

ASH→ PESTO PEPPERS→

DUE TO THE POPULARITY OF EUROPEAN CHEESES, MANY OF THEIR DAIRIES GOT OVERRUN AND THE CHEESE SUFFERED. MANY AMERICAN DAIRIES ARE STILL SMALL AND GROOVY. TRY 'EM!

YOU'LL DO GREAT!

CHAPTER 9

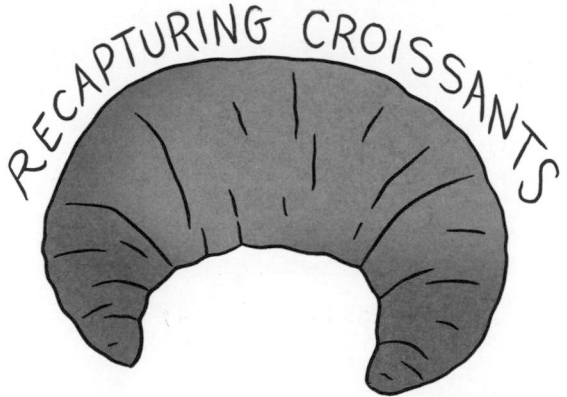

RECAPTURING CROISSANTS

The summer after my freshman year of college, my best friend, Nelly, and I bought Eurail passes and went backpacking through Europe.

Deux, s'il vous plait.

Billets

We didn't have any money, but we didn't particularly mind.

Let's hear it for student museum discounts.

Hear, hear.

We stayed in cheap hostels, and spent what little we did have on museums and food.

Try these!

This is the best chocolate ever.

Our weird hostel in Barcelona, with cubby beds

We ate well, knowing that in a few weeks, we'd be back to ramen noodles and hot dogs.

We're a little under-dressed for this place...

Oh well. Yum!

I remember so many delicious meals from that trip, but nothing holds a candle to the memory of the croissants from a tiny Venice bakery.

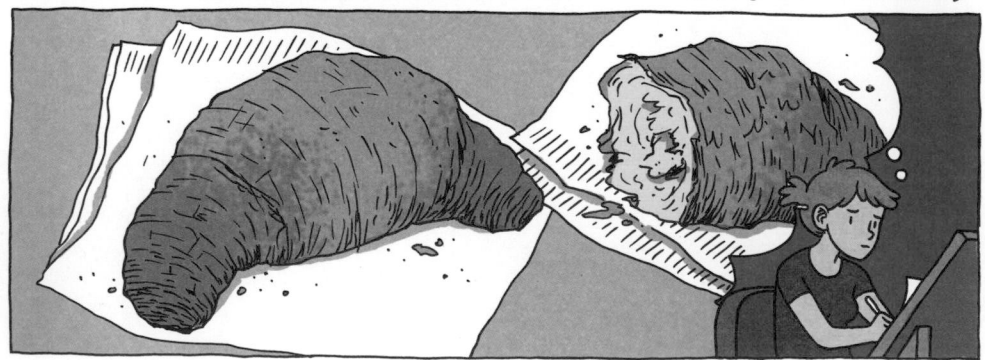

Our hostel in Venice was a strange little place, with overlapping rugs and the smell of the canal drifting up to our bedroom window.

They charged for the use of the hot water knob, so we showered cold, grateful that it was a warm July.

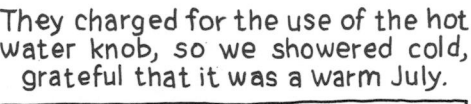

The first morning, I could smell the bakery over the mossy canal smell.

Nelly sleeps later than I do, so I ventured out alone to investigate.

The bread and chocolate smells emerged from the bakery in waves of intoxicating warm air.

Inside, the croissants were coming out of the oven in gleaming rows, fragrant and appealing despite the oppressively humid morning heat.

I bought two, for Nelly and me to eat for breakfast.

I chose to eat mine on the hostel steps, so I could watch the gondolas bob as I ate.

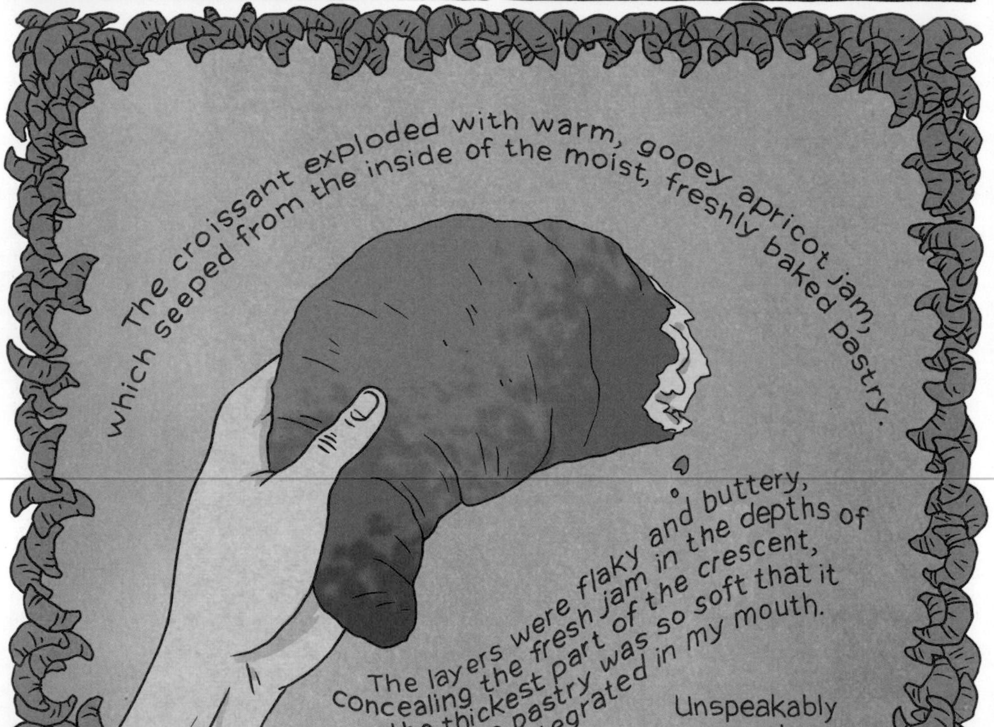

Grazie.

Prego.

The croissant exploded with warm, gooey apricot jam, which seeped from the inside of the moist, freshly baked pastry.

The layers were flaky and buttery, concealing the fresh jam in the depths of the thickest part of the crescent, where the pastry was so soft that it nearly disintegrated in my mouth.

Unspeakably good.

I had eaten both croissants before I could stop myself, and had to return to the bakery.

I bought four more, and ate three.

Later, I brought Nelly her croissant.

She's very bleary in the mornings...

...But still, she knew.

The next summer, Nelly and I were living in a small apartment in Chicago.

It ain't Venice, but the rent is cheap!

July rolled around, as hot as it had been in Venice, and I began to think of that bakery, and those croissants.

I think I'm gonna try to bake those croissants we had in Venice!

Neat.

She never appreciated them as much as I did.

Jeez.

Don't get excited, or anything.

(In another misplaced food adventure from our trip, Nelly favored cumin-y potato samosas, bought warm from a vendor on a beach in Spain.)

My craving began an obsession. For weeks I tried to re-create the croissants, trying recipe after recipe, to no avail.

Nelly would return from work to find every available surface of the apartment covered with pastry sheets of cooling croissant failures.

I could never quite get it right — the heat from the oven in our un-airconditioned apartment made me delirious, and my failure was frustrating.

That elusive flavor was unattainable.

Nelly put a stop to my repeated attempts after a few weeks, thankfully.

And reluctantly, I put my quest on hold for the time being.

But still, the mysterious deliciousness of those croissants continues to haunt me. I suspect that the ingredient I lacked in Chicago was the anticipation and delight of waking on a morning of possibilities, far from home and school, in an ancient, watery city.

Then again, maybe that odorific canal water had something to do with it. Who knows?

I still think of them, especially in the summertime: golden and light, with sweet tea and butter, flaking apart to reveal the yellow jam inside... Like eating the Venice sunlight.

MAKING CROISSANTS IS **HARD.**

I'M SERIOUS. I'VE TRIED SO MANY WAYS, ALWAYS WITH IMPERFECT RESULTS.

cheating! Wheee!

YOU KNOW WHAT'S GOOD, ACTUALLY?

THAT CANNED DOUGH YOU CAN BUY AT THE GROCERY STORE!

POP

WAY LESS CLEANUP!

FUN NOISE!

PRETTY DECENT RESULTS!

SO, THAT SAID, SORRY — NO CROISSANT RECIPE. HOW ABOUT ONE FOR:

 # SANGRIA

INSTEAD?

RED WINE
(OR GRAPE JUICE)

SPARKLING WINE
(OR SPARKLING APPLE JUICE)

LEMONS

APPLES

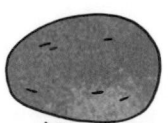

MANGO

PEACHES

ORANGES

WATERMELON

(GET WHAT YOU CAN/LIKE, DEPENDING ON THE SEASON.)

IN A BIG JAR WITH A LID:

SQUEEZE ORANGE & LEMON HALVES, THEN TOSS THEM IN.

2-3 CUPS RED WINE ~OR~ GRAPE JUICE

POUR

3 CUPS SPARKLING WINE ~OR~ SPARKLING JUICE

MAKE SURE YOUR JAR'S LID SCREWS ON

TO KEEP IN THE FIZZ!

CUT OTHER FRUIT INTO QUARTER-SIZED PIECES & ADD.

FOR AN EXTRA KICK, ADD SOME BRANDY OR LIQUOR. (PEACH BRANDY IS NICE.)

FOR A NON-ALCHY VERSION, TRY A BIT OF MAPLE SYRUP INSTEAD!

LET SIT in FRIDGE for ABOUT 24 hrs.

STRAWS HELP.

SERVE COLD IN THE SUN.

BE SURE TO INCLUDE A SPOON SO YOU CAN EAT ALL THE FRUIT!

AND BE WARNED!

IT'S DANGEROUSLY YUMMY!

CHAPTER 10

DINING
with
Zeus
&
Demeter

For someone who claims to love food, my father's fridge is strangely empty.

He is the king of condiments, though. His pantry is full of things like lonely jars of pink peppercorns, fancy mustards, and various types of relish.

He prefers to be served – excellent food at a nice restaurant, preferably at a zinc-top bar with a glass of wine.

It was lucky that he stayed in New York City when my parents split up. He could step around the corner to any one of hundreds of restaurants in his neighborhood.

While my mother found new ways to connect to the growth and preparation of food in the country, my father allowed his stove to collect dust.

My father appreciates nice things: tasty wine, good books, and excellently prepared food. He lives in lovely comforts, occasionally beyond his means, and he can always be counted on to eat well (and to feed me well).

My paternal grandpa had a handful of heart attacks by the time he was sixty.

He's a sweet man who grew up on a chicken farm, which put him off eating poultry for life. (Even at Thanksgiving!)

By the time he was the age that my father is now, his diet excluded all red meat, butter, and salt.

Not so for my father, who does Pilates and looks ten years younger than he is.

But he loves to eat—he misses my mother's cooking, and takes any opportunity—birthdays, graduations, homecomings—to enjoy it.

My mom's boyfriend, Paul, is a picky eater.

He's also a vegetarian.

He had a recurring nightmare where he stood before an animal tribunal.

He prefers to cook for himself, which is a source of contention between him and my mother, who expresses herself through her cooking.

I was thinking of making yummy pesto!

I'll just make myself some stir fry.

His vegetarianism isn't about health. His diet tends toward the pizza and doughnuts variety of vegetarianism.

My mother has pretty much given up on her attempts to cook for him, as each new dish she prepares is usually refused in favor of soy-sauce-doused rice.

Cooking separate meals, together

For my mother, a rejection of her cooking can be seen as a rejection of her affections.

But when I come home to visit, Mom pulls out the stops and we cook lovely things together every day!

I sometimes feel like the Persephone to her Demeter— returning to herald her feasting celebration of harvest.

Demeter is the goddess of the harvest.

Persephone is her daughter.

In this metaphor, my father would be Zeus, the maladroit king who is served in the city of the gods.

It's not a perfect metaphor, but it's pretty good...

Demeter & Zeus

Goddess of agriculture and nature

Used to be together, but aren't anymore

Resides on Olympus, the home of the gods

Lives in nature

They have a daughter

Likes the ladies

Powerful independent woman

Has two brothers

As a result of being daughter to a man who is served like a king, when we see one another, we usually dine out!

Welcome to— Oh!

Patrick!

Le Zinc

One time, Dad read about the food in Vancouver, and decided to go.

We ate sweet Kusshi oysters from the cold Pacific, and cured salmon on dill sourdough toast.

The best meal we had all week was seared halibut, crispy on the outside and perfectly plain and fresh.

My father spent all week expounding on the purported delights of the city's most hyped restaurant, at which we had reservations for our final night in town.

But when that night arrived, the food was TERRIBLE. The fresh seafood drowned in saccharine sauces, inedibly overcooked and ridiculously garnished.

The king was displeased.

When we got back to the States, Dad drove me to Mom's house for a visit, in the hopes that she'd make a welcome-home meal for us.

Maybe she'll make pesto!

Or Mexican food!

He wasn't disappointed, as she's always happy to have her cooking so loved and appreciated.

My mom's yard actually has a tree with a bricked-in heart-shaped hole!

Come in! I'm making stacked enchiladas!

We had my mother's stacked enchiladas with homemade mole and fresh queso fresco, green salsa, and black beans.

crema

cilantro

onions

As he plowed through the food, like it might disappear, I realized that while my dad might eat well, his fancy restaurants are just a poor substitute for the regular gig he once had.

No matter the inventive techniques or the freshness of the fish— the well-designed interior and zinc bartop, all the hype and awards...

They'll never live up to the pleasure of dining at my mother's table.

Summer Pickle Recipe

1. PICK A BUNCH OF CUKES FROM MOM'S GARDEN (WATCH FOR SLUGS!). GREEN ONES ABOUT THE LENGTH OF YOUR HAND ARE BEST FOR PICKLES.

2. WASH OFF THE GARDEN DUST, THEN STABBITY-STAB EACH CUCUMBER A FEW TIMES. (THIS LETS THE BRINE SOAK IN EASIER)

3. COMBINE IN A LARGE POT:
   - ½ GALLON APPLE CIDER VINEGAR
   - ½ BOTTLE OF PICKLING SPICE
   - 1 TSP OF MUSTARD POWDER
   - ½ TSP OR A SPRIG OF DILL
   - ½ AN ONION (CHOPPED)
   - 2 TBSP SALT

4. BRING TO A SIMMER, THEN TOSS IN THE CUKES. (DON'T ACTUALLY THROW THEM!)

PLOP

Cover, to keep in Pickliness!

A FEW GRAPE LEAVES ADDED TO THE BREW IS SUPPOSED TO MAKE THE PICKLES CRUNCHIER!

⑤ COOK ON MEDIUM (COVERED) FOR ABOUT 15-20 MINUTES (GET READY FOR YOUR HOUSE TO SMELL LIKE PICKLES).

SNIFF

⑥ POUR THE MIXTURE INTO A BIG CERAMIC VAT THAT YOUR MOM USUALLY USES TO HOLD SPOONS.

PICKLE STEAM

PiCKLeS!

⑦ WAIT ABOUT 24-36 HOURS, THEN DO A TASTE CHECK.

⑧ JAR THOSE SUCKERS!

LUCY'S PICKLES

Are you Pickles yet?

A note on pickles:

MY GRANDMOTHER MADE INCREDIBLE PICKLES.

MY MOM TRIED TO DUPLICATE THE PROCESS, TO NO AVAIL.

ALWAYS PERFECT MAKEUP AND PEARLS

Sigh.

Perfect!

(MY MOM WAS A COOKING WIZ, EVEN AS A TEENAGER, BUT THIS WAS MY GRANDMOTHER'S SPECIALTY.)

SHE'D BUG THE VENDORS AT MARKET TO PICK THEIR CUKES EARLY SO THEY WERE TINY AND FLAVORFUL.

SHE HAD SOME VAGUE, MYSTERIOUS RECIPE THAT WAS SOMETHING LIKE:

IMPOSSIBLE TO RE-CREATE!

- COVER WITH WATER
- ADD 1 HANDFUL SALT
- 1 HANDFUL SUGAR
- ONCE A DAY
- FOR ONE WEEK
- THEN ONCE A WEEK
- FOR ONE MONTH

NOBODY'S REALLY SURE.

MY GRANDMOTHER DOESN'T EVEN REMEMBER.

MAYBE IT REQUIRES YOU TO WEAR **PEARLS** IN ORDER TO GET IT RIGHT.

WHEN MY MOM AND DAD MOVED TO NEW YORK CITY JUST AFTER THEY WERE MARRIED, MY MOM DECIDED THAT THEIR TINY APARTMENT WAS THE PERFECT SETTING TO LEARN HOW TO *PICKLE EVERYTHING.*

GIANT PICKLE CROCKS IN A TINY APARTMENT

THEIR COAT CLOSET NEVER SAW COATS.

STILL, MOM NEVER QUITE GOT MY GRANDMOTHER'S RECIPE JUST RIGHT. MAYBE I'LL BE THE ONE TO DO IT SOMEDAY!

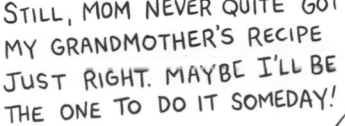

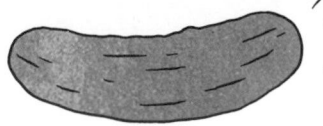

PICKLE JUICE RUNS IN OUR VEINS.

CHAPTER 11

When Bad Food Happens to Good People

People who know me, or know my mother, sometimes worry about feeding me. I'll be invited to dinner with the preamble:

I know it's not your mother's cooking...

In the present age of widespread food obsession, lots of people are pretty confident about what tastes good, but plenty of people don't give a fig about food.

No thanks...

Because my mother is a professional chef, and her cooking is legendary, friends assume that I'm spoiled when it comes to food (possibly true, but not in the way they might think).

My mom is a chef!

My mother cooked for strangers all the time, so she was rarely interested in cooking around the house.

Can we have tacos for dinner?!

On a regular night at home, I'd more often find myself picking at leftovers from her catering events, or she and I would stand at the kitchen counter and eat cherry tomatoes from the garden as a substitute for dinner.

A Typical Dinner

Milk

cereal →

Cherry tomatoes

When someone cooked, it was an EVENT. I *love* being cooked for.

Who Doesn't?

I love the treat and pleasure of eating when it becomes an act of focused giving and sharing.

Good restaurants manage to emulate this act of generous creativity. Bad ones try, at least.

I'm fascinated and confounded by friends who claim "food is just fuel."

Whateverrr...

I always picture zombies, shambling toward any old bag of meat.

I'll eat iiit...

who caarres?

Food isn't important

My younger cousin was, and continues to be, a picky eater.

Red meat and bread, only.

How have you possibly grown to adulthood?

Picky eater stories are amazing!

I only eat fast food.

cheese flavored snacks.

I've never had a single green food.

They make us appreciate the many wonderful foods we eat and how different every appetite is.

My enthusiasm for food might have earned me a little reputation among my friends' parents...

The only thing that could possibly give *me* cause to refuse a meal is the addition of

Miracle Whip:

The one definitive tasty-killer that will ruin *everything*.

But it's pretty rare for me to dislike a meal, with a few exceptions...

During graduate school, my friend and classmate Mark was learning how to cook.

THE WORST MEAL

He'd never been away from his mother's cooking, and finally he was forced to learn how to feed himself.

From what I can tell, he subsisted on a pretty typical grad student diet...

But Mark wanted to really cook.

Unfortunately, his source for recipes was the internet: such a vast and unedited collection of personal tastes that any sort of specific guidance is essentially nonexistent.

1. Fish Biscuits — Time: 40 min combine fish paste with...
2. Make your own White Castle Sliders — Prepare...
3. Ham Puffs — Love ham? love whipped cream? Well...
4. Lemonade Chicken — First

Unaware of good cookbooks or reputable recipe websites, he clicked randomly until he found something that looked impressive but manageable.

This experimentation resulted in a series of meals that have since become both a legend and a cautionary tale.

The worst of these, known as "lemonade chicken," was easily the worst meal I've ever (tried) to eat.

Ham Puffs — Love h
ove whipped cream? Wel

Lemonade Chicke
Buy a bunc spices tha

Potato and Orange Ca
abbage in this dish! We

The liquified fried rice

Hot dog lasagne

The Lemonade Chicken!

It involved at least twelve expensive spices, never to be used again, and the repeated dousing of frozen lemonade concentrate while cooking.

That memorable meal being the unpleasant exception, I love to be cooked for. The pleasure of eating food prepared by friends, or preparing food for friends, lasts much longer than the bad taste.

This served both to pack the chicken full of artificially saccharine citrus flavor, like a lollipop-flavored chicken...

...And to ensure that the frozen temperature of the concentrate chilled the chicken and prevented it from ever becoming fully cooked.

So... This is the worst.

Ha ha! Yes.

Simpler is usually better when it comes to cooking for people. Tons of spices or difficult ingredients can overwhelm good food. Just remember the triumvirate:

Mark made a valiant effort. It's not hard to be a good cook, even if you're not naturally inclined, but it helps to know a few tricks...

FOUR NEAT-O TRICKS TO REMEMBER WHEN YOU COOK:

1. Rehearse Before Opening Night

If you wanna make something special, do a practice run to make sure you know how to do it, any tweaks to make, and how long it takes.

2. Cook Meat Fully

Chicken should reach at least 165° to be fully cooked & safe to eat.

Invest $5 in a meat thermometer.

Steak's done-ness can be judged by feel. Compare the texture to your hand:

RARE — LOOSE FIST
MEDIUM — TIGHTER FIST
WELL — TIGHT FIST

3. Have an Ol' Reliable

Have a good meal that you've got down pat. Practice until you get it.

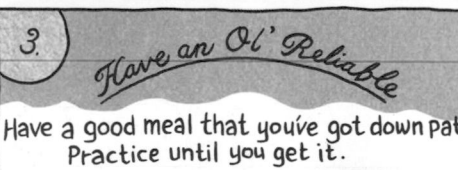

Knowing how to cook one thing perfectly (like a chicken) can help teach you to cook other things (and give you a speciality!).

4. When in Doubt, Potluck

Inviting guests to contribute food lets them partially "own" the meal, and helps them appreciate the effort in cooking for others.

I can't say I really enjoyed eating Mark's creation, but I certainly loved the gesture, and it will always remain an enjoyable meal in my memory.

Not least because he's a perfectly capable cook now, and I can tease him about it forever.

Wasting money and appetite on bad food is disappointing, but it doesn't matter when the company is good.

Eating is generally a solitary act; absorbing the flavors with your own particular preferences...

But there's a lot to be said for eating as a social act.

It's a treat, even when the food is bad.

SHEPARD (FAIREY) PIE

IN ART SCHOOL I HAD TO WRITE A PAPER ON THE STREET ARTIST, SHEPARD FAIREY. YOU KNOW:

BECAUSE I ~~WAS~~ AM A BIG NERD AND I LIKE SHEPARD FAIREY, I DID MY PAPER EARLY, SO WHEN FINALS ARRIVED, I WAS THE ONLY ONE OF MY CLASSMATES WHO WASN'T TOTALLY NUTS.

YES!

SHADDUP

ART SCHOOL FINALS ARE PRETTY BRUTAL.

EVERYONE WALKS AROUND COVERED IN PAINT AND CHARCOAL DUST. NOBODY SLEEPS, AND EVERYONE EATS THINGS ONE SHOULD NEVER EAT... WHEN/IF THEY EAT.

MICROWAVE DINNERS

MOST OF A JAR OF PEANUT BUTTER, STRAIGHT

A WHOLE SLEEVE OF COOKIES

THIS ONE SAVED FOR BREAKFAST

SO MANY ENERGY DRINKS

(YOU ALSO EAT QUITE A LOT OF ART SUPPLIES, BY ACCIDENT.)

SO HAVING BEEN SPARED FROM THIS DESERT OF NUTRITION THIS TIME, I THOUGHT:

I'M GOING TO MAKE SOMETHING TO FEED MY CLASSMATES.

STILL COVERED IN PAINT AND CHARCOAL

ZZZ

WEEP

FOOD IS HAPPINESS, COMFORT, ENERGY, AND ~SOMETIMES~ A NICE BRIBE.

LIKE ME!

1. SAUTE SEITAN IN OIL WITH CHOPPED ONION.

SIZZLE

2. PEEL AND BOIL POTATOES

(3-4 BIG ONES SHOULD DO.)

GLUB

3. CUT UP CARROTS,* ZUCCHINI & MUSHROOMS.

X3   X1   *PEEL FIRST!   X 10-20

4. MASH POTATOES (WITH MARGARINE, TO KEEP IT VEGAN, AND S&P).

I DIDN'T HAVE A MASHER IN COLLEGE...   ...SO I USED A FORK.

5. LAYER IN BAKING PAN:

MASHED POTATOES →
FROZEN PEAS/CORN →
CARROTS/ZUKE/SHROOMS →
SEITAN →

X-RAY PAN

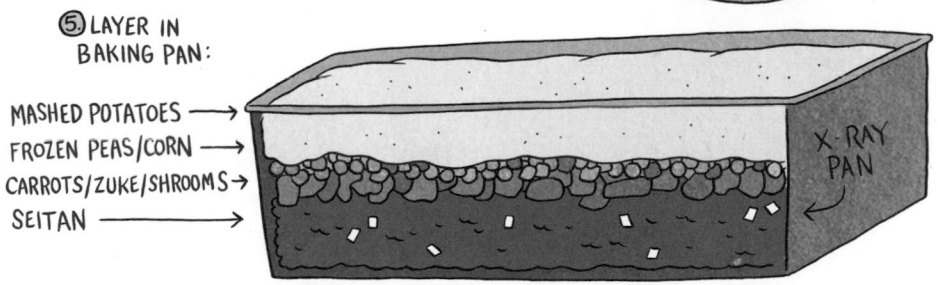

6. BAKE ON 400°F UNTIL TOP IS A BIT BROWN AND CRISPY.

7. LET COOL (AT LEAST AN HOUR), TAKE TO CLASS, ABSORB LOVE.

PRO TIP #1:
SPOONS ARE BETTER THAN FORKS FOR THIS. EMAIL AHEAD TO ASK PEOPLE TO BRING A SPOON AND BOWL TO CLASS.

SNARF   OM NOM

PRO TIP #2:
ADDING SOME AVOCADO IN WITH THE VEGGIE LAYER IS DELICIOUS! (IT WAS TOO RICH FOR MY COLLEGE BUDGET.)

CHAPTER 12

MOLECULAR GOOD-BYE

After almost eight years of living in Chicago, I realized:

I'm homesick.

I went halfway across the country for college, and stayed. Chicago was new and exciting, the food industry booming, and the city mine to discover, out from under the shadow of my mom and dad.

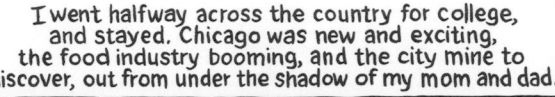

I loved the city and its intricate neighborhoods and sprawling space, so different from where I'd grown up.

But after these past two years, writing about my memories of my childhood and adolescence in New York, I began to come back around.

SIGH

New York City

Catskill Mountains

I wanted to discover New York like I'd done with Chicago. A new and old place at once, different from the perspective of adulthood.

And I missed my mom's cooking.

SIGH

Before I left Chicago, there were a lot of good-byes to make...

HOT DOUG'S

APPLE, PEAR & PORT ELK SAUSAGE WITH CHERRY FIG MUSTARD, CARAMELIZED ONIONS & SMOKED GOUDA

MIKO'S ITALIAN ICES!

BANANA CHOCOLATE → ← KIWI

urban belly

ASIAN SQUASH & BACON DUMPLINGS

molly's cupcakes

SUN WAH

Soft bun

Peking duck

Veg

KUMA'S CORNER

Blue cheese

Apple

walnuts

Dried cran-berries

Bacon

BURGER The "JUDAS PRIEST"

SULTAN'S FALAFEL

The Logan Square Farmers Market

"Lucila's" alfajores

"Nice Cream" Tea & cookies mini cone

"Fonda del mar" Uchepos

Banger Sand-wich

"Spencer's Jolly Posh"

LONGMAN & EAGLE

Warm gruyere donuts, fig jam, hazelnut mascarpone & wild flower honey

WOW BAO

Coconut custard bao

BBQ PORK bao →

REVOLUTION BREWERY

Leek, apple, and cider blue cheese mussels

and ALINEA

Rabbit sausage

Smoking oak leaves

Three years before my last summer in Chicago, I'd saved up and gone to Alinea with my then-boyfriend (now close friend).

After years of drooling over the articles I'd read about it, the catalyst came when I read the biography of Alice Waters that credits Alinea as being the top restaurant in the country.

Blah blah Michelin blah

Usually pretty irritated by restaurants with long waits or high prices, I waited the two months for our reservation for the $250 prix fixe with anticipation.

FEBRUARY

That meal is hard to describe, even with explicit details about the food.

Pillow that steams Lavender-scented air

Sous vide duck

DUCK CONFIT

Grilled duck

Mango

YOGURT

The whole restaurant is organized around exposing all senses to the process of enjoying yourself.

If a restaurant is like a pleasant Ferris wheel, Alinea is like a super-intense roller coaster.

AUG!

AAAH!

BACON, SUSPENDED WITH SUGAR STRANDS

I wrote about the meal in a comic, for fun and to remind myself of the adventure I'd had on this rare occasion of luxury.

(It might surprise you that a comic artist who occasionally still takes cater-waitressing jobs doesn't usually have $250 to spend on one dinner.)

A few weeks after my comic went up online, I was e-mailed by Nick Kokonas, the co-owner and founder of Alinea, who thanked me for the comic and invited me to someday tour the kitchens at the restaurant.

In my last, delicious summer in Chicago, I knew I needed to cash in that favor.

Dear Nick,

Hey, remember me?

I don't know what this is, but it smells AMAZING! Like mushrooms. Balsamic. Burn. Lemon.

Test-tube holder

Strange items bubbling on a hot plate

These faces are INTENSE.

Cloth carefully placed and then lifted — to remove skin?

This mixer was bigger than my head!

Delicate hands

Gelatin stuff!

Rubbing something through a sieve

Dishwashing grimace

GRANT ACHATZ!

(I recognized him from his flippy hair)

Pasta?

90° angle

Bandaged

Nick Kokonas

163

On the way home from the kitchen, I was awed and humbled. After a whole youth enmeshed in the food industry, I'm still such a neophyte. Just a groupie, backstage at a rock concert.

It's nice to be so excited by things, and to know I'm not alone in it.

I was right next to the plating area!

cool!

These days there is a huge culture of people who are excitedly learning to connect with and love food in new ways.

It's especially exciting in America, where food hasn't always been a major part of our culture, like it is in France, for example.

Bad habits or industrial compromises have forced many of us to reexamine our relationship to food and begin to embrace eating as a connection to our bodies and a form of celebration.

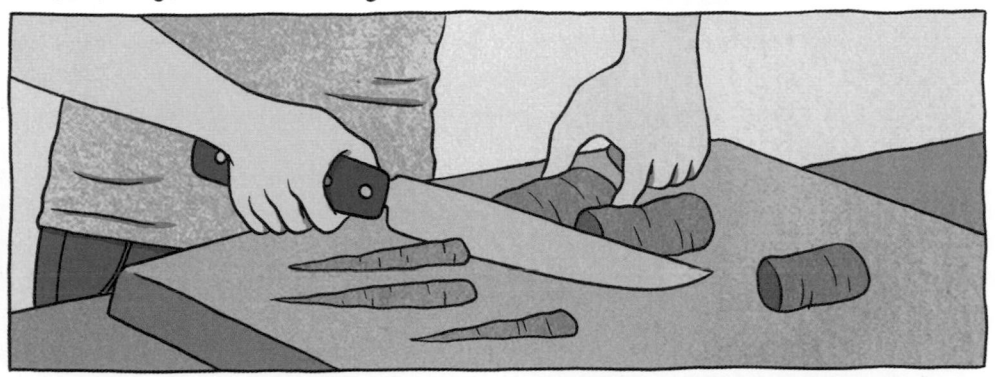

We're still a young country, discovering new things, creating traditions of eating and sharing.

Like me, still a young woman, learning about what moves me, what I want. What I love.

SIZZLE

TOSS

And doing those things with excitement, curiosity, and *relish*.

"And looking at one single label on a jar,
he felt himself gone round the calendar
to that private day this summer when
he had looked at the circling world
and found himself at its center.

The word on the jar was RELISH.

And he was glad he had decided to live."

−Ray Bradbury, "Dandelion Wine"

THE END

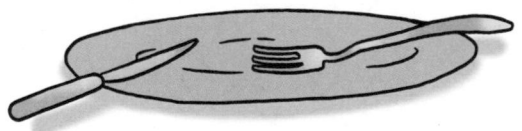

AFTERWORD

(Me, helping in the kitchen)

To research this book, I dug through my family photos for reference.
Sifting through the pictures of cheese plates, pies, turkeys, and canning projects,
I found some actual *human* subjects in the mix!
So here's a little photo album about the book that you just read.

I really did spend a lot of time on the kitchen counter as a baby. It's a good thing my mother is retired from catering now, or I'm sure she'd be in trouble for health code violations involving my feet in the flour.

Pretty!

Infused vinegars Mom made

My uncle Peter's store was a lovely little food spot. It was part of an early 80s wave of gourmet food in New York City. I love this photo of him at work in the kitchen at his old store.

gross

The mysterious spice rack

The big butcher block

My friend Drew features in a couple of these chapters. He and I have been lifelong friends, and we've shared a lot. Here we are sharing a marshmallow.

More recently, sharing the kitchen.

My mom is really the star of these stories. She has taught me so much about food, cooking, and the power behind the act of feeding oneself and others. Here she is in the kitchen of our old New York apartment.

My kitchen wasn't quite as well-equipped, but it was still pretty great. I had an array of plastic menu items. I think it's pretty clear how much I have always revered my mom.

My mom and I moved to the country when I was around eight. I missed the Chinese food in New York, but I was won over by the picnics.

Eventually, I got into it. Here we are at the county fair, where my mom's fancy pumpkin won the *highly* coveted "award of merit" (basically proof of participation of any sort). Frankly, I think my mom's fanny-pack should have won a FASHION prize.

NIce TRY.
AWARD OF MERIT
DUTCHESS COUNTY FAIR
RHINEBECK NEW YORK

Helping in the garden. Or, at least, posing like I'm helping in the garden.

My mom and me with two of our chickens. The one on the left is Miss Demeanor and the one on the right is Toepecker. May they rest in cantankerous peace.

One of Mom's farmers market stands.

I helped out at my mom's farmers market stands for years, selling fruits and vegetables and cheese and flowers at markets around the Hudson Valley.

Here's me "helping out" by very obviously eating the blueberries we're supposed to be selling...

...And here's me "helping out" a few years later, by very obviously reading a book behind the table (I was probably on a break!), and hiding my eye under awkward adolescent bangs.

My mom is cool.
She's always been cool.

Tracing the stories back, it's amazing seeing how the connections form to bring us to here and now—the parallels with my own life and the events that could have only happened to her.

My mom uses food to teach, to understand, to make connections to herself and others, the way I use drawing and writing.

Which is why it's great that I get to combine these elements in a book that tells our stories—about cooking and eating and growing up with a love for food and stories and cool coincidences.

I hope I did her justice!

A very well-worn picture of Mom fluffing the front displays, when she first started working at Dean & DeLuca in the 70s.

My grandmother, the pearl-wearing pickle-whisperer

My mom as a kid in the kitchen

Mom and Dad, soon after they moved to New York City

Five years before I was born, in the neighborhood where I'm writing this now

Nice pants, Dad.

First Second
New York & London

Copyright © 2013 by Lucy Knisley

Published by First Second
First Second is an imprint of Roaring Brook Press,
a division of Holtzbrinck Publishing Holdings Limited Partnership
175 Fifth Avenue, New York, New York 10010

Cataloging-in-Publication Data is on file at the Library of Congress

ISBN: 978-1-59643-623-7

First Second books are available for special promotions and premiums.
For details, contact: Director of Special Markets, Holtzbrinck Publishers.

First edition 2013
Design by Colleen AF Venable
Printed in China

10 9 8 7 6 5 4 3 2 1